SINGAPORE
PERSPECTIVES
Politics

SINGAPORE PERSPECTIVES
Politics

Edited by

Natalie Pang
Shamil Zainuddin

Institute of Policy Studies, Singapore

iPS Institute of
Policy Studies

LKY Lee Kuan Yew
School of Public Policy
National University of Singapore

World Scientific

Published by

World Scientific Publishing Co. Pte. Ltd.

5 Toh Tuck Link, Singapore 596224

USA office: 27 Warren Street, Suite 401-402, Hackensack, NJ 07601

UK office: 57 Shelton Street, Covent Garden, London WC2H 9HE

British Library Cataloguing-in-Publication Data
A catalogue record for this book is available from the British Library.

SINGAPORE PERSPECTIVES
Politics

ISBN 978-981-122-768-4
ISBN 978-981-122-572-7 (pbk)

For any available supplementary material, please visit
https://www.worldscientific.com/worldscibooks/10.1142/11979#t=suppl

Desk Editor: Sandhya Venkatesh

Contents

Preface

JANADAS DEVAN

Some years ago, IPS Fellows decided to focus on four areas of research: diversity, aging, income inequality, and the governance of a city-state. As part of its focus on the fourth area, IPS has returned, over and over again, to the question of politics — the science or study of government and the state, to use one of the many definitions of the word in the Oxford English Dictionary. Significantly, if we examine the deep history of the word, we will find that it comes from the Greek word *polites*, or "citizen"; and *polites* in turn comes from another Greek word, *polis*, or city.

Fortuitously or not, we might say that politics has been a particular concern of citizens of city-states. Singapore, being about the only successor in the modern era to the Greek city-states, is naturally, concerned about politics. The topic is of course timely. The organisers of Singapore Perspectives in 2020 settled upon it for that reason.

Another reason is that 2021 will be the 10th anniversary of Prism, a scenario-planning exercise that began in 2011 on the question: "How will Singapore govern itself in 2022?" It was one of the most ambitious projects that IPS has ever embarked upon. More than 140 people from seven key sectors of society — from corporate leaders to public intellectuals, from the public service to civil societies — were asked to develop scenarios of Singapore's possible political trajectory from 2011 to 2022. In 2012, the various scenarios imagined were presented through forum theatre and interactive exhibits put together by Drama Box and Mr Kok Heng Leun.

I will do no more than recall here the three scenarios that Prism settled upon. The first was called "SingaStore.com" — *singa* as in "lion", and *store* as in a place where you buy things. This scenario envisioned a "pro-business, high-growth world that the public trusts, which invests in people and endeavours with the highest potential to create economic value". The question was how socially sustainable such a world would be.

The second scenario was called "SingaGives.gov", as in "to give" things. This was envisaged as a pro-Singaporean scenario where the public trusts in a new government and an elected president to implement an egalitarian framework supported by the use of the national reserves. The question here was how fiscally sustainable such a Singapore would be.

The third scenario was called "WikiCity.sg" — *wiki* as in "Wikipedia". This was envisaged as a pro-active scenario with a new coalition government elected to trim the role of the states — because citizens had come to have low trust in government — and which would allow for self-organising communities to emerge to meet the daily needs of the people. The question here was how politically sustainable such a society would be.

I leave it to you to judge how prescient the 140 Prism participants were. Possibly the scenarios say more about their state of mind in 2011 than they do of the future, which is now almost present. Undeterred, nevertheless, we will embark on yet another scenario-planning exercise soon, a sort of Prism 2, around the question: "How will Singapore govern itself in 2032?" Singapore Perspectives 2020, we hope, will suggest profitable lines of enquiry.

Politics is not simply about political parties. The question of what "good politics" looks like for Singapore is one that *all* of us need to engage with. It was Zuraidah Ibrahim who defined our greatest political challenge as how can we change and yet remain together. Deputy Prime Minister Heng said something similar: How do we remain together, while being part of an exceptional city-state? Be well-organised, never stop thinking of tomorrow and yet accommodate greater political diversity, plurality and a greater contestation of ideas.

Acknowledgements

IPS is grateful to the following institutions
for their support of Singapore Perspectives 2020.

GIC

Keppel

PONTIAC LAND

TEMASEK

Introduction

NATALIE PANG AND SHAMIL ZAINUDDIN

Immerse the audience in our colourful political history .... It does not have to be very rosy; it does not have to be all about a single party. There are many paths taken by individuals in political parties, civil society and non-governmental organisations, which have brought us to where we are today.

The quote above is from a brief that we wrote during an initial meeting on the theme "Politics", for Singapore Perspectives 2020 (SP2020). Should this conference be about electoral politics? Should this conference highlight pivotal choices that individuals from various political parties and civil society have made? Should this conference be about the past or the present?

We concluded that a Singapore Perspectives conference on the theme of "Politics" would present a wide variety of views, not just from the perspectives of parties and the geopolitical influences shaping Singapore's politics, but also perspectives of citizens that are making changes in new ways. We wanted an engaging event that would allow attendees to build on the past while deliberating about the future. So serious were we about wanting to "immerse" the audience in Singapore's politics that we wanted to explore an experiential multimedia event where images and videos of key moments in Singapore's political history would be projected on all the walls of the conference room. Numbers and space were not in our favour, so we redirected our focus and resources to curating dialogues and panels that would present a diversity of opinions and personalities — personalities who were not only authorities in their chosen field but who were also engaging speakers. SP2020 sought to engage the audience in a reflective dialogue on their "experience" of politics, both in the traditional sense of elections and governance as well as beyond those formal structures.

Being researchers, we are acutely aware of the impact of politics on the public and that it is not just the realm of a select few. The panels created were meant to reflect a broader and more inclusive definition of politics. That was the reason why we created two panels — one that examined the role of political parties and geopolitics in shaping the political landscape in Singapore, and another that looked at how non-governmental actors especially younger citizens contribute to our polity.

The first panel forms Section I of this book and looks at the political landscape of Singapore focusing on the paths taken by different political parties, as well as the impacts of geopolitics on Singapore. This section is therefore titled "Paths Taken". Our esteemed authors write not only about the dominance of the People's Action Party in politics but also the opposition and various challenges faced. Historian and President of Yale-NUS, Professor Tan Tai Yong writes of the challenges PAP faced after right after Singapore became independent, their (the PAP's) opponents had different ideas and chose different approaches, but a combination of circumstances and political miscalculations led to the weakening of the opposition, which gradually lost potency as a political force. In Chapter 2, political scientist and Principal Research Fellow at the East Asian Institute, NUS, Dr Lam Peng Er picks up on the topic of challenges and trajectories of the PAP. He argues that a large part of the success of the PAP and thereby Singapore is due to revolutionary ideas of late former Prime Minister Lee Kuan Yew and his "lieutenants". He repeatedly refers to them as "revolutionaries" who promised and delivered policies and ideas that formed the lasting foundation on which Singapore is built on. In his chapter, and on the topic of where PAP is heading, Dr Lam cites Duverger's theory — which states "all dominant political parties are doomed to fall from power" — and examines whether that will be PAP's fate as well. Providing a sharp analysis on opposition party politics, Deputy Executive Editor of the *South China Morning Post*, Ms Zuraidah Ibrahim cites in her chapter "three constants" and "three unknowns" to sum up the opposition. From arguing that the opposition is "not a government in waiting" as being one of the constants to the unknown of how economic and geopolitical conditions will influence voters, her chapter successfully sheds much light and clarity to the seemingly opaque world of opposition politics in Singapore. Chairman of the Middle East Institute, NUS, Mr Bilahari Kausikan picks up on the impact of geopolitics in Chapter 4, titled "Fatalism is Fatal for Small States". He discussed lessons learnt from the merger and eventual separation with Malaysia and agreed with Dr Lam Peng Er that it was the rare blend of "political skill and technocratic competence" of our first-generation leaders that allowed Singapore to be relatively more successful than many countries which gained independence around the same time. We hope that the chapters in Section I provide useful lessons to readers interested in political history, leadership and governance.

In Section II, titled "New Forms and Movements", we look at other important actors in politics. The authors in this section are people leading and studying grassroot movements, initiatives and non-governmental organisations. As the influential anthropologist Margaret Mead stated, "Never doubt that a small group of thoughtful, committed citizens can change the world: indeed, it's the only thing that ever has." It is an argument that Associate Professor Farish A. Noor of the S. Rajaratnam School of International Studies, might agree with, judging by his context-setting essay. From child labour to humour, he sets the scene about how much societies have changed and the importance of the people advocating for it. Youth advocates and scholars spoke about and for various issues ranging from migrant workers, single mothers, the environment and social media. On the latter, Principal Research Fellow at Curtin University A/Prof Crystal Abidin wrote about her work studying social media and its impact. From influencer culture to meme factories, she showed, amongst other things, how these actors and their tools could be used as forms of resistance against social issues like racism or homophobia. Someone who has committed himself to address social issues especially relating to migrant workers is Director of Citizen Adventures, Mr Cai Yinzhou. He spoke of the work of Citizen Adventures and how he worked with communities to enact change. He organised and led tours in Geylang neighbourhood to share with others how he views his home and challenges stereotypes of the place being a crime-ridden area. He also described serving migrant worker neighbours by offering free haircuts and reminded us that we should, "talk *to* one another, and stop talking *about* one another." This theme of empathy resonates in Ms Carrie Tan's chapter as well. As the founder of Daughters of Tomorrow she advocates for women, especially single mothers or as she put it, she helps "un-helpable women". In Chapter 7, she wrote about her work with these resilient women and how she worked with the organisations like AWARE and government bodies to bring about change. In the final chapter of Section II, Ms Nor Lastrina Hamid, Co-founder of Singapore Youth for Climate Action detailed the different phases and players in the climate movement in Singapore. She also made a plea for all to put aside our differences and work together to save the environment.

We organised two dialogues – the first with Deputy Prime Minister (DPM) Heng Swee Keat (See Chapter 1) and the Second with Minister Chan Chun Seng (See Chapter 9). DPM Heng talked about bringing the people of Singapore together. He spoke of the important work to ensure "differences do not become entrenched, and corrode social cohesion." As for Minister Chan, he presented three hypotheses "to keep Singapore going, growing and glowing", in the midst of local and global challenges.

We had also envisioned a dialogue session with Mr Pritam Singh who is by now, the Leader of the Opposition after the General Election in July 2020. Unfortunately, Mr Singh declined the invitation. We were however fortunate and honoured that representatives from other political parties accepted our invitation and that they made full use of the Q&A sessions to engage our speakers with a variety of questions. We captured some of these moments and other selected questions from students, civil servants and people all walks of life in the final chapter of this book, "Key Moments of Q&A".

Lastly, it would be interesting to note that the Singapore Perspectives 2020 event might not have been. Held on 20 January 2020, it was three days before the first confirmed case of COVID-19 in Singapore. Looking back at January while writing this chapter in the second half of 2020, one would get a sense that the world will not be the same post-pandemic. On top of that, Singapore had a general election in July, which saw an increase in the number of opposition members being elected to Parliament. The general election also saw one of the authors, Ms Carrie Tan, elected successfully as Member of

Parliament. So much has changed that we decided to invite our authors to write a short reflection on their experiences post-SP2020. Not all the authors decided on writing a post-script, but the ones who did like Dr Lam Peng Er, Ms Zuraidah Ibrahim, Ms Carrie Tan and Ms Lastrina Hamid, reflected on key events in 2020 and whether their opinions, predictions, conclusions still stand.

While the Singapore Perspectives 2020 conference ended in January 2020, we hope you see this book as a way of continuing the dialogue on politics in Singapore.

We would like to thank all of our esteemed chairs and speakers for their outstanding presentations, chapters and exchanges with the audience during the conference. The IPS administration team is the finest we have ever worked with, and we will always be grateful for they have been instrumental in ensuring that the event carried out smoothly. It is not often that one has the luxury of focusing on planning the programme, engaging the speakers and chairs the way we did, but we were able to do so with their support. Lastly, we would like to thank our copy-editor Wenshan for improving the readability of this book.

CHAPTER 1

Singapore, Together

HENG SWEE KEAT

The three Singapore Perspectives Conferences I have attended in 2014, 2016 and 2018 were respectively themed "Differences", "We", and "Together". "Differences" have come to define politics today. Across the world, existing fault-lines have deepened, and have been exploited. This has in turn put stress on the sense of "We", stressing social cohesion and weakening mutual trust. In many places, this has severely undermined society's ability to forge a common path forward.

As Singapore is not immune from these pressures, the key imperative for our "Politics" should be to manage our "Differences", expand our common purpose to engender a greater sense of "We", and ensure that society can progress as one — "Together". I will address each of these themes in turn.

"DIFFERENCES"

Over the last decade, many countries have seen their political consensus fracture. The state of the world did not use to be this way. After the Second World War, the major players in the world forged a new global order, based on the ideals of multilateralism, the market economy, and free trade. The expansion of trade and investment enabled economic growth at an unprecedented pace. Advanced economies led the charge on global economic growth and globalisation, while cascading technology, skills and capital to the developing economies. Global trade boomed, investments poured into developing economies, and billions of people saw their lives improve. Singapore is one of those countries that has benefitted significantly from globalisation.

But the last decade has shown that not all countries have kept pace with the changes confronting them. In some societies, globalisation has exposed workers to greater competition, while technological advancement has disrupted jobs and livelihoods. The developed world is feeling the competition, as a number of developing economies, including those in Asia, move rapidly up the value chain. In some instances, these countries have leap-frogged the developed world in areas such as e-commerce and e-payments. Income and wealth inequality have grown, and the consequences have been more severe for countries that have failed to restructure their economies and upskill their workers. Societies with rapidly ageing populations are feeling the strain, because many pension plans are underfunded, and welfare spending is at an unsustainable high.

The ripple effects of these changes have resulted in many people becoming anxious and resentful. They have become increasingly pessimistic about their future, and upset about the lack of progress in life, they have amplified much of their discontent on social media, in narrow silos and echo chambers. More worryingly, they have come to view their governments and institutions with distrust.

This has ushered in an era of "anti-politics". Insurgent political parties — including far right parties — have exploited these fears and frustrations for their own political gain, campaigning along nativist and protectionist lines, and further undermining trust in public institutions. These divisive forces have washed over many societies, including Europe and Latin America. In the United States, bipartisan consensus over important issues has evaporated as the Democrats and Republicans each move to shore up their own base ahead of elections at the end of the year. And in Asia, it has been more than seven months since mass rallies and violent protests erupted in Hong Kong.

While we have fared better than most, we are not immune to the same divisive forces that have swept across the world. In fact, we have already seen some semblances of nativist tendencies here in Singapore, such as some of the public discourse around foreigners. If we do not act decisively, and if we allow these forces to creep up on us, our hopes and concerns can be exploited to create fear and anger. Our diversity can be turned against us. Our unity can fray, and our society can wither.

Therefore, as we close the decade, we need to make sure that differences do not become entrenched, and corrode social cohesion. We should also be mindful of the dangers of political parties using divisive rhetoric to gain support in a fractured landscape, and the risks of falling prey to the pull of populism. We cannot assume we will be immune.

"WE"

This brings me to the second word: "We". Amidst these disruptive forces, can Singapore be different? Can Singaporeans strengthen our sense of "We" in the coming decade and beyond?

The notion of "We" as citizens of Singapore is relatively new. We are a young nation, and as our Bicentennial last year reminded us, our present existence as a successful, sovereign nation is a historical anomaly. That is because for most of our history, this place was a part of larger kingdoms. We were buffeted by global and regional forces, and our fate was determined by powers beyond our control.

Eventually, our self-determination set us on a different course. We became an independent nation, and we were able to find success as one united people. There are two key questions here: "How did our forefathers beat the odds, and turn an island of mudflats into a multicultural metropolis?" and, "What must we do to keep our nation successful and sovereign?" I believe a strong sense of "We" was key to this. Our improbable success was made possible by exceptional governance — capable leaders, working together with a united people.

In the decades after Independence, our founding fathers fostered a sense of nationhood by introducing policies that gave people a stake in Singapore. They welcomed foreign investment and decided on the path of rapid industrialisation, creating jobs for the tens of thousands of young Singaporeans, and enabling people to provide for their families. They invested heavily in education, and ensured each generation had more opportunities than the last. For example, only 22 per cent of those born in the 1940s received post-secondary education. For young Singaporeans today, that figure is more than 95 per cent. Through their housing policies, our founding leaders turned a city of squatters and slums into a nation of homeowners in just a few decades. Together, these policies meant that every Singaporean, regardless of race, language or religion, had a chance to live well, age well, and a chance to make the future better for their children.

This shared experience of progress united the founding generation of Singaporeans, and strengthened the trust between the people, and the government. Over time, a virtuous circle was established. The government had a strong mandate and was able to never stop planning for the future. They realised their bold political vision through sound, sustainable policies. In turn, Singaporeans trusted their leaders, because they saw their lives improve in real ways, and they had a strong sense of optimism for the future. This nurtured the trust between Singaporeans and the government, and this gave them the confidence to make sacrifices for the greater good, and for future generations. This is the formula behind our success, and this has kept Singapore exceptional.

This approach must remain core to the government's mission, especially as we grapple with longer-term issues facing us. In an era of rising inequality, we will strengthen our fundamentals, and ensure no Singaporean is shut out of opportunities because of their family circumstances. This is why we have been increasing our investments in pre-school education, and doing more to level up children from disadvantaged backgrounds. In an age of disruption, we will step up efforts to encourage lifelong learning for our workers. We are currently developing the next bound of SkillsFuture, and we will make a further push to help workers pick up new skills, and to seize new opportunities. One such group is those in their 40s and 50s. Some among them completed their education more than two decades ago, and might not have had the opportunity to upskill.

In a period of widening generational divides, we must continue to give hope to our young. Public housing will continue to remain accessible and affordable to all Singaporeans. As our people live longer and our society ages, we will take care of older Singaporeans. Our seniors should not only have a roof over their heads, but also have enough for retirement and their healthcare needs. The Pioneer and Merdeka Generation Packages were tailored to help older cohorts meet their healthcare needs for life. The upcoming Budget will help lower and lower-middle income Singaporeans, including current and future seniors, to meet their retirement needs in a sustainable way.

Our unity as a nation, and as one people, has been strengthened by our sense of shared mission. This was not achieved by closing ourselves off to the world, or by looking inward.

As we turn our gaze to the next decade and beyond, we must continue to be creative and agile in charting our way forward, and we must stay open and connected. This is especially because in the coming years, we will be confronted by the continued strategic competition between the United States and China, and an even swifter pace of change in the nature of jobs and the economy. In addition, there is the rapid ageing of our society, and the increasing manifestation of existential threats, like climate change. But there are bright spots. Southeast Asia is growing rapidly geographically and culturally, and we are in a good position to contribute to the region's growth. More broadly, we are also well placed to serve as a node between Asia and the world. As a small island nation, we are nimble. We are ready to innovate, test-bed and scale new solutions. In this way, we can continue to stay relevant to the world, and because we are small, and non-threatening, we can be friends with all, even in a turbulent world. This is how we can turn our constraints into opportunities, and create opportunities in the face of disruption.

The way ahead will not be easy, but you have the unwavering commitment of the government, and from the 4G leadership. My colleagues and I will make every effort to build a future of progress for Singaporeans in the coming decades. A future where we can continue to prosper as a nation, where all Singaporeans have opportunities to succeed. A future where the benefits of progress will be shared with all, where no one will be left behind if they give their best. A future where we pull together as one, turning our differences and diversity into our strength.

"TOGETHER"

The differences and divisive forces I described earlier will continue to challenge our notion of "We", our national identity and our sense of rootedness.

Apart from these forces, Singaporeans ourselves are also becoming more diverse in terms of our needs, aspirations and views. Singaporeans born after Independence do not share the bonds of war and struggle that the Pioneer and Merdeka Generations experienced. The digital era has allowed for an exchange of diverse perspectives. But there has also been a proliferation of more extreme opinions, and a narrowing of views in echo chambers. Our demographic profile is also changing. Last year, more than one in three citizen marriages involved trans-national couples.

In the face of all these changes, it is now even more crucial to maintain our sense of who "We" are as a people; focus on what we have in common; and work "Together" to build our shared future.

How do we do this? We must first make sure that we continue to have strong political leadership. This means having political leaders of integrity, who are deeply committed to the wellbeing of Singaporeans and the future of Singapore. The political leadership must have the trust and support of Singaporeans. They must also have the ability to craft strategies to take Singapore forward, amid the seismic changes around the world, and to partner our people to deliver outcomes. They must have the moral courage to do what is right for the people, and not just what is popular. We cannot be all things to all people.

Since our independence, Singaporeans have worked together with their political leaders to turn an improbable nation into a land of opportunities. We must continue to do the same, by strengthening trust between the government and the people, and also among Singaporeans.

In this regard, what I learned during the 2012 Our Singapore Conversation (OSC) exercise was both instructive and heartening. OSC was not just a forum for the younger leaders to better understand the aspirations and concerns of Singaporeans, but also a platform for Singaporeans to hear and better understand each other's perspectives.

My experience working with Singaporeans showed me that they understand the trade-offs and the need to make hard decisions for the collective good. They are also willing to find common causes, and work together to overcome the odds, to make the impossible possible. This collective "can-do" spirit has been forged over the decades, as we faced challenges together. Time and again, crisis after crisis, we have shown that every Singaporean will rise to the occasion and do his or her part, and that no one will be left behind.

Some may not think much about what we have achieved together. But I believe that our people can see, understand and draw their own conclusions. They can see that this government will always strive to understand their needs and concerns, work hard to address them, and deliver on our promises. We are upfront about the hard truths facing Singapore, and also about our mistakes, even if they are politically inconvenient.

Nevertheless, in a society increasingly flooded by information and misinformation, it is critical that we find ways to deepen understanding and relationships among our people, and to redouble our efforts to maintain a balanced perspective. We must reject extremist views that will fray our social fabric, and be discerning about falsehoods and irresponsible promises that cannot be fulfilled. Most importantly, we must find new ways to come together, reaffirm what we hold in common, and work collectively towards a shared future.

This is why I launched the Singapore Together movement in June 2019. I believe that each of us can make a difference, and by acting together, we can make a bigger difference, and achieve what may seem daunting or impossible. My 4G colleagues and I are committed to go beyond just working for you, to working with you, to build our future Singapore. We want to mobilise the passion, creativity, and can-do spirit of Singaporeans, as we find common cause, experiment with new ideas and solutions, and beat the odds together. I will highlight a few areas of this movement.

CO-CREATION: DESIGNING AND SHAPING OUTCOMES TOGETHER

First, we are opening up several areas for Singaporeans to get involved in designing policies, and putting them into action. We started new platforms, like the Citizens' Panel and Citizens' Workgroup, where we engaged Singaporeans on their ideas on making different aspects of life better, such as improving work-life harmony and encouraging household recycling. The ideas are well thought-out, and we are working to put their ideas into action.

We are also involving Singaporeans in directly shaping our physical environment. These include the Somerset Belt, our parks, and also the Geylang Serai cultural precinct, which I visited over the weekend. Singaporeans of all ages will have a hand in developing ideas, evaluating the options, and shaping the eventual designs.

On this note, I was very happy to find out that in the "New Forms and Movements" section, you will get to read about change makers like social entrepreneur Mr Cai Yinzhou, Ms Nor Lastrina Hamid — who is passionate about tackling climate change, as well as Ms Carrie Tan, who founded the charity Daughters of Tomorrow almost a decade ago. I hope their sharing will inspire all of us.

Second, we have also been making a more concerted effort to engage Singaporeans on the upcoming Budget. Recently, I attended a session with youth leaders and we explored the challenges and opportunities for Singapore, and how we can partner one another to create a better future for all. It was a rich learning experience for everyone, and I certainly learnt a lot.

Third, Singaporeans are also sharing their ideas about making our home a better place, and putting these ideas into action. During our Bicentennial year of commemoration, I attended many events by various religious groups, clans, schools, businesses, and charities. I learnt so much about the imagination and commitment of each group, to uplift the lives of people they are serving. Businesses are also doing their part. In a span of three short years, the Company of Good initiative has grown into a network of more than 1,400 companies. This network has enabled companies to learn from one another, to form partnerships, and to bring corporate giving to the next level. Many Singaporeans are letting their actions speak for themselves. Total volunteer hours have increased from 45 million hours in 2008 to 122 million hours in 2018, and under SG Cares, there are many more opportunities to contribute than before.

CHALLENGES

Singaporeans are gradually taking charge and doing good, at all levels of society — each in their own way mobilising the people around them to make Singapore a better place. The creativity, energy and commitment of our people are most inspiring.

It encourages us to take the next step, to invite Singaporeans to tackle bigger "Challenges" and seize more "Opportunities" in the coming decades. Some are existential — like addressing climate change and rising sea levels; others are issues that can benefit from a fresh approach, such as how we can keep our seniors active and healthy, as our lifespan increases.

There are many possibilities for us to work together, such as keeping Singapore safe and secure, developing the full potential of our people, growing our economy to create more opportunities and resources for our people. Or making sure Singapore will become a green, sustainable, and liveable city, and building a caring and cohesive community.

CONCLUSION

These are the early days of our Singapore Together movement. What we see forming is a new model of partnership, between government and Singaporeans in owning, shaping and acting on our future. In this process, government agencies are learning to develop and deliver policy solutions in a more collaborative manner. At the same time, Singaporeans too, are gaining a deeper appreciation of the challenges and trade-offs in making national policy. And collectively, we are learning to understand different viewpoints, to distinguish truth from falsehood, and to find a way forward in the midst of diverse and often conflicting opinions. The government will continue to exercise leadership in areas where we are expected to, such as in security and defence, and in ensuring that we plan and act for the long term.

Above all, I am confident that our partnership efforts to date will set the foundations for the work of a generation. Just as our founding leaders made home ownership their cornerstone policy to give Singaporeans a stake in Singapore and a share in our progress, Singapore Together will be our new cornerstone of nation building; a way of working that reflects and strengthens our shared ownership of Singapore's future.

Our approach to politics and governance has served us well over the past 55 years. As we embark on a new decade, we will face a world marked by "Differences". As a small nation, we will be buffeted by these forces. We must continue to work with like-minded countries to bridge divides between countries, and to tackle global common challenges. There is no doubt that our sense of unity as one people and our cohesion as a nation will be tested. But I am confident that going forward, Singapore can continue to excel and thrive, and shine brighter as a little red dot.

"Singapore, Together". This is our way forward. Our way of ensuring that we progress together, and that the benefits of progress are felt by all Singaporeans. Our way of harnessing our diversity as strength, so that we are greater than the sum of our parts. Our way of creating a shared future and finding common ground, so that we remain united as one people. Our way of ensuring Singapore remains exceptional, as we ride the winds of uncertainty and waves of disruption.

I invite all Singaporeans to join us on this journey, as we continue to chart our shared future together.

Paths Taken

Introductory Remarks

TAN TAI YONG

Let me begin by making reference to a book that was published more than 10 years ago. In 2007, a group of scholars brought together a collection of essays on the political history of Singapore in the 1950s/1960s in a book called *Paths Not Taken*. The essays dealt with the theme of political pluralism in post-war Singapore, when there was a ferment of ideologies, priorities, perspectives, as well as different social visions for the future of Singapore. Coming from a spectrum of varying political interests, these visions often contested and conflicted with one another. The volume offered an interesting scholarly and intellectual exercise on the question of "What if?" What if different paths had been taken by Singapore at that critical juncture before independence and the country had to move on a different trajectory?

While the objective of this section is not to discuss "what if", it will analyse the political landscape in Singapore by examining the paths that were actually taken. The paths ahead for Singapore were indeed quite clear in 1965 when being part of Malaysia was no longer an option. Having to leave Malaysia in 1965, Singapore had willy-nilly become a sovereign nation state. The PAP (People's Action Party) government had a sense of what it wanted to do, had to do. Their opponents had different ideas and chose different approaches, but a combination of circumstances and political miscalculations led to the weakening of the opposition, which gradually lost potency as a political force.

While the PAP government seemed to be dominant domestically by the late 1960s, it had to contend with larger geopolitical forces that would shape the thinking, approaches and directions of the young country. So, the paths and options that were taken from 1965 were also shaped by a combination of political decisions, historical experience, circumstances of the time, as well as chance and geopolitics among other factors. What lie behind the paths taken at that time, therefore, warrant closer study and analysis, if only to better understand the situation we are in today and what changes we can expect in the future.

We have three experts who will share their insights and analysis on several of these issues in this section. Dr Lam is a political scientist and Principal Research Fellow at the East Asian Institute at the National University of Singapore. He is a noted scholar of Japanese politics, but has also written extensively on Singapore and is the co-editor of an important book titled *Lee's Lieutenants*. Dr Lam will discuss the roles, choices and contribution of Singapore's Old Guard and reflect on the development of the PAP in the present and near future.

Ms Zuraidah Ibrahim is currently Deputy Executive Editor of the *South China Morning Post* in Hong Kong. She was previously Deputy Editor of *The Straits Times*, and also has written very extensively on Singapore politics. She co-authored the book *Lee Kuan Yew: Hard Truths to Keep Singapore Going*, published in 2011, and also a monograph on the Singapore opposition, published in 2017. Zuraidah will discuss the development and contributions of opposition parties in Singapore's politics and, in a similar vein, reflect on their development and the future of Singapore's opposition parties.

Mr Bilahari Kausikan was the Permanent Secretary of the Ministry for Foreign Affairs from 2001 to 2013, and has held various positions in the ministry and abroad including post of Singapore's Permanent Representative to the United Nations in New York and Ambassador to the Russian Federation. He is currently the Chairman of the Middle East Institute at the National University of Singapore. Bilahari will discuss how Singapore's politics had been shaped by and are shaping relations with our immediate and distant neighbours. He will provide perspectives on developments in the context of this relationship, and how he sees Singapore politics evolving in the near future.

CHAPTER 2

The PAP: Past, Present and Future

LAM PENG ER

IPS (Institute of Policy Studies) instructed me to do two things: first, to analyse the roles and the legacy of Lee Kuan Yew and his key lieutenants; and second, to examine the trajectory of the PAP, past, present and future. So, my chapter will be Janus-faced, looking both backward and forward. The analogy is driving a car — we look ahead and anticipate the future, we also look at the rear mirror, and reflect on the past.

ON LEE'S LIEUTENANTS[1]

The die was cast when the founding fathers set the template of good governance in Singapore. They established the values and ideals of meritocracy, non-corruptibility, multi-culturalism and ethnic equality. Indeed, these are wonderful ideals. We are a young nation — still a work in progress. Singapore has not attained such values perfectly, but can we name any countries in Southeast Asia doing better than us on such values? Certainly, all the Southeast Asian countries are multi-cultural but in terms of meritocracy, non-corruptibility and ethnic equality, have any done better than us?

I don't mean to be hubristic. But many Singaporeans have already embraced and

> Heng Swee Keat is an ethnic Chinese Singaporean but what about his successors? Can we have a non-Chinese Prime Minister? Is it conceivable? Is this desirable? This path is open ended at the moment.

---

[1] See *Lee's Lieutenants*, edited by Kevin Y.L. Tan and Lam Peng Er, published in 1999 and revised in 2018.

internalised these values. And the logical extension and marker of these values in the years ahead for the PAP and Singapore is to have a capable non-Chinese Prime Minister. Heng Swee Keat is an ethnic Chinese Singaporean but what about his successors? Can we have a non-Chinese Prime Minister? Is it conceivable? Is this desirable? This path is open ended at the moment.

The Old Guard, or founding fathers, made a virtue out of necessity. They harnessed the dynamism of international capitalism, embraced an open economy and attracted foreign investment. This developmental strategy was very critical to create jobs for the masses — good jobs essential for political and social stability. But they actually tempered it with socialism too. These socialistic benefits for the masses included affordable housing, education and healthcare. And Singapore's equivalent to fundamental land reforms is the superb public housing programme, which created property-owning working and middle classes. So, we have avoided the unhappy fate of Hong Kong where housing for the masses is relatively unaffordable.

I argue that Lee and his lieutenants were revolutionaries — it was a bloodless revolution from above: public housing, nation building to forge a national identity within one generation, national conscription, bilingual language policies. They were very contentious indeed. The founding fathers pushed them through and these are their crowning achievements. They were indeed revolutionaries, but what about the 2G, 3G, 4G leaders? By and large, they are technocrats — providing technocratic leadership. You may think they are reformers or not. Arguably, they fine-tuned the system and kept the flag flying. Singapore's style of governance may change, but the fundamental values remain essentially the same.

DEFYING DUVERGER'S HYPOTHESIS

I spent a lot of time in mainland China, and my Chinese friends talk about the Singapore model (新加坡模式). We have trained more than 55,000 mainland Chinese officials in Singapore. That's simply remarkable. Kim Jong Un came to Singapore for his summit with Trump, and he was at Marina Bay Sands. He remarked, "Singapore's social order is very good, it can be a point of reference for DPRK (Democratic People's Republic of Korea)." So, this is our Singapore.

But what about the future in a turbulent world? Maurice Duverger, a French political scientist, had a very interesting hypothesis. He theorised:

"The dominant party wears itself out in office, it loses its vigour, its arteries harden. It would thus be possible to show that every domination bears within itself the seeds of its own destruction." So, is it a done deal that the PAP will still be the ruling party two or three decades from now?

The PAP seems to have defied Duverger's prediction thus far. Look at the Congress Party of India, a perennial party in power during its halcyon days — but no more. Across the causeway, UMNO (United Malays National Organisation) was in the opposition. The party that I spent a lot of time examining, the Liberal Democratic Party of Japan, was in power from 1955 till 1993, went out, then back in power in 1994, and between 2009 to 2012, it was in the opposition. Is the PAP going to be the last dominant electoral party in the world? The other grand old dominant parties — the PRI of Mexico, KMT of Taiwan and the Christian Democrats of Italy, have all fallen.

The puzzle is this: why did the PAP succeed in maintaining one-party dominance since 1959? On this question I am sure everyone has different views. I would argue that it's the quality of the PAP leaders, its ability to attract talent and the smooth passing of the political baton. That's why we have 2G, 3G and 4G leaders in systematic renewal. Moreover, the institutions, norms and blueprint of governance established by the Old Guard still resonates with the electorate. If these values were not embraced by Singapore's citizens, I think they would have been thrown out of office. Successful economics stewardship indeed. I dare say, that for the majority of voters in Singapore, they do find life in Singapore rather tolerable, very good for many on the whole, even if there are unhappiness with specific public policies such as public transportation and immigration policies. But on path dependency and paths not taken, I have no time to talk about the strategic blunder of the opposition Barisan Sosialis, which boycotted the 1968 general election and gave the PAP a monopoly of Parliament and power.

Looking at the 2011 general election results, the opposition captured almost 40 per cent of popular votes, but did not win as many seats in Parliament. This is the consequence of the first-past-the-post electoral system, which worked to the advantage of the ruling party.

The other thing to note, is that the PAP is very impressive at the grassroots. If we talk about Lee as the captain, and the Old Guard as his lieutenants, then who are the sergeants and the warrant officers? They are the PAP MPs (Members of Parliament), at the grassroots, down at the trenches.

They work really hard. If you have any problems, you can go and see and consult your MP. I don't think you will leave empty handed if you are truly in need. Moreover, the PAP is a very disciplined cadre party; it's not faction ridden.

The advantage of a perennial rule by the PAP is its symbiotic ties with state machinery, National Trades Union Congress (NTUC), a strong influence on media, and the extensions of its hegemonic values to society. Many Singaporeans embraced the values articulated by the Old Guard. As an incumbent party, it's fairly autonomous and not beholden to lobby groups like the big property developers in Hong Kong.

BATTLE FOR THE FUTURE

What is the road ahead? I am actually not unduly worried about the financial power of Singapore, even though there may be a lot of anxiety and fear mongering by some Singaporeans. We have more than sufficient reserves for our population of 5.7 million. If we have the political will and if state and society can forge a national consensus, surely, we can deal with the homeless of slightly more than 1,000 people.

So, the PAP, which have fought the politics of survival so well, our separation from Malaysia in 1965, must address the politics of aspiration and identity among our diverse, better educated, younger and cosmopolitan electorate.

On the future of PAP — they can prudently dip into the national reserves for a rainy day and win electoral support. But under our constitution, you need the consent of the elected president and the Council of Presidential Advisers to draw on the reserves if need be, in the wake of black swan events, domestic challenges and external threats. So, we do have the financial wherewithal to weather crisis.

And from Deputy Prime Minister's discussion and questions raised from the floor, we are cognizant that Singapore's society will be more pluralistic, more global, diverse in values and interests in the years ahead. The question is: can we maintain unity in diversity? Is this a motherhood statement — seeking unity in diversity without leading to fragmentation and fissures in our society? Obviously, the PAP must evolve and adapt. Likewise, for the opposition parties too. So, the PAP, which have fought the politics of survival so well, our separation from Malaysia in 1965,

24

must address the politics of aspiration and identity among our diverse, better educated, younger and cosmopolitan electorate.

The PAP has calibrated its public policies. It has shifted from a neo-liberal market-oriented mentality, especially in the 1990s, to a somewhat more socialistic approach after the 2011 general election. I think the PAP has responded well to the electorate to stay in power. It has actually offered more generous benefits from national coffers to the working class, older workers and retirees, better housing subsidies, rise in bursaries, grants for preschool and tertiary education, goodies for the Pioneer and Merdeka generations including healthcare subsidies — all these are genuine benefits for Singaporeans indeed.

Here is some food for thought on the PAP's hegemonic control of political narratives and facts. POFMA (Protection from Online Falsehoods and Manipulation Act) was mentioned a few times during this conference. Will it be effective? Can you imagine in future elections, if you have opposition parties, civil society and individuals making all kinds of statements, how are we going to police and enforce it? Will the High Courts be overloaded? Are we going after them selectively? Certain things are obviously black and white. But in life, there are 50 shades of grey. Who decides what is true or not? Will we be caught in an X-files situation where the truth is somewhere out there? And it's up to the High Court judge to decide what is fake and what is real? In principle, POFMA may be necessary but implementation, I am not sure. It's too early to tell.

On the PMET (Professionals, Managers, Executives and Technicians) problem, how are we going to address rising social inequality? Social inequality is endemic in the world. Oxfam notes that there are 7 billion people in the world, but 50 men control more than 50% of the global wealth. Is that not problematic and vulgar? Singapore is so globalised. Can we escape from global trends of widening social inequality?

Can political parties attract the support of millennials? My daughter is a millennial and she thinks very differently from me. Will the PAP leadership remain united in the post-Lee Hsien Loong era? What will happen when he steps down as Prime Minister? Will he be a Senior Minister and then become a Minister Mentor? Can PAP afford a Team B without splitting, without tearing itself apart?

Back to 1955. What was the population size of Singapore then? In 1959, when PAP became the ruling party, when Singapore attained self-government, the population size of the country was under 2 million, and most citizens lacked tertiary education. We now have a population of 5.7 million, and one that is better educated. Can the PAP draw on this larger pool of talents for a Team B?

Now, this may be a bit controversial: political elitism. I will qualify it by saying that I have not come across any political systems in the world where there are no elites. It's a matter of degree, but in the case of Singapore, can the PAP's governance evolve from a small elite circle to greater political participation and transparency in governance? Let citizens know, for example, the approximate value of our national reserves?

And yesterday was very interesting when we read *The Straits Times*. According to the figures from the United Nations Department of Economic and Social Affairs, 44 per cent of our foreign migrants come from Malaysia while 18 per cent were from mainland China.[2] It's quite strange for a Singapore citizen to hear this from the United Nations, rather than from the government of Singapore. Can citizens, civil society and opposition parties have better access to information? It's not just helping hands but thinking heads that are necessary for nation building. We do need accurate information for informed deliberation and consensus building.

Can a small political elite circle make mistakes? Yes indeed — just look at the electoral backlash in the 2011 general election over immigration, housing and transportation. Uncharacteristically, Prime Minister Lee Hsien Loong apologised. He apologised for mistakes made in public policy. We have a very good civil service, intelligent MPs, good ministers among the best paid in the world, but mistakes can still be made. So, in the years ahead, is there an inherent danger for the PAP and Singapore, if a small elite circle were to make major mistakes? Is it unthinkable, inconceivable? And are we all putting our political eggs in one basket? What if a future PAP Team A were to fail, is there Team B or Team C?

---

[2] Published on 19 January 2020, the article, titled "Migrants in Singapore Mostly from Malaysia", noted that "the UN figures reveal for the first time, where migrants in Singapore were originally from."

This term, "natural aristocracy", came from Prime Minister Lee Hsien Loong when he spoke to Fareed Zakaria in 2015. But when he talked about the natural aristocracy, he said it must be earned, it doesn't mean that natural aristocracy is being born with a silver spoon in your mouth. So, my question is: will the PAP's so-called "natural aristocracy" in the future be based on the nobility of character, rather than the privilege of birth and political dynasties?

I am a Japan specialist. We know that around one third of the Lower and Upper House Members of Parliament come from political dynasties. And in the future, Koizumi Shinjiro may become Prime Minister after Abe Shinzo and his immediate successors. Koizumi Shinjiro, the son of former Prime Minister Koizumi Junichiro, is a fourth-generation politician in democratic Japan. So, what about Singapore? Are we going down that route? Is that going to be the path taken?

What are the more formidable political challenges to the PAP? There are a number of opposition party members here in this conference. I think you can answer this question better than I. Can you, dear members of the opposition, attract talent in greater numbers and offer a narrative that counters the PAP's hegemonic ideological discourse? If you don't have a message, you don't have a story, and you cannot attract people. You cannot just blame the PAP for repression, for propaganda and so on, so I think that's the way to go — recruit good people to join your opposition parties.

And a trillion-dollar question: Can the PAP, in the decades ahead, avoid Duverger's theory and prediction that all dominant political parties are doomed to fall from power? I reiterate, all dominant political parties eventually fall out of power. Is that the fate of the PAP? It may not be so apparent today, maybe they will be around in power for a decade or two; but beyond that, I wish I can ask you guys to take a vote. But I am sorry, I am not clairvoyant, so I cannot answer the question.

POSTSCRIPT ON GE2020

In GE 2020, the perennial party in power, the PAP, continued to defy Duverger's theory that all dominant parties will eventually run out of vitality and fall. The PAP captured a solid 61.2% of the popular votes and a lion's share of the electoral seats. At the Singapore Perspectives Conference, I noted above that Singapore under the PAP's economic stewardship has accumulated substantial reserves for a rainy day. Indeed, the city-state has the wherewithal to draw down on its financial reserves to tide over the black swan COVID-19 "thunderstorm". I also flagged the problems of widening social and economic inequality, and a narrow circle of elites and "natural aristocrats" in Singapore. Unfortunately, COVID-19 has accentuated unemployment and inequality in Singapore. The debacle of Liew Mun Leong, then Chairman of the Board of Directors of Changi Airport Group, enraged many Singaporeans who felt that Liew, as a top and well-connected elite, blatantly abused his asymmetry of power by falsely accusing his vulnerable domestic helper of theft, which is a jailable offense. In September 2020, this debacle became a lightning rod of mass anger against the perception of elite arrogance in Singapore. If the PAP were to become a casualty of Duverger's theory, it might well be due to mass anger and perceptions of an insufferable and self-seeking political and economic elite class in Singapore. Simply put, if a future PAP were to move away from the public spirit of the Old Guard, then it may well fall from power. In this regard, the 4G leaders cannot rest on the laurels of their predecessors but must forge a new social contract based on meritocracy (not aristocracy), multiculturalism, justice and equality with a new generation of Singaporeans.

CHAPTER 3

Singapore's Opposition: Surprises or More of the Same?

ZURAIDAH IBRAHIM

We know from past elections that they always show up surprises, defying the pundits; it may look like an issue-less election weeks before the campaign, indeed someone told me over dinner this weekend that the only issue that seemed to matter was PMDs (Personal Mobility Devices). But things can change rather quickly. We also know that the opposition, 11 of whom are here, I am told, are good at keeping their cards close to their chests. Think back to how well the Workers' Party's Mr Low Thia Khiang guarded the secret of him leaving his safe perch of Hougang for the Aljunied GRC (Group Representation Constituency) contest in 2011.

THREE CONSTANTS

Despite these uncertainties, we can identify a few givens about the opposition, as well as a few known unknowns, so to speak. I will highlight–three relatively stable factors that I believe are unlikely to change in the coming election. They are not big surprises, but are useful to know to frame our discussion.

First, the opposition are not a government in waiting. Furthermore, that's not what most voters expect from them. They function as a potential check on the ruling party, a means for citizens to exert pressure on the PAP government. In this sense, Singapore is fundamentally different from a full two-party or multi-party system where elections are about political parties vying for their turn to rule. Instead, we have a dominant party system, with

Nevertheless, many voters will continue to use their vote as a way to deliver a desired level of check and balance, rather than to decide who should govern Singapore for the foreseeable future. That is a known issue. So, although every election is a guessing game, most of the speculation is simply about exactly what level of accountability Singaporeans seek during a particular election cycle.

government, while opposition parties reflect Singaporeans' desire to impose a certain level of accountability on that government. That is not going to change in 2020.

The dominant party context helps explain why most voters do not expect the opposition to have fully formed platforms with detailed policy proposals. The PAP, understandably, finds this very frustrating. It has criticised such voting behaviour as irresponsible and keeps warning that this is opposition for opposition's sake. Nevertheless, many voters will continue to use their vote as a way to deliver a desired level of check and balance, rather than to decide who should govern Singapore for the foreseeable future. That is a known issue. So, although every election is a guessing game, most of the speculation is simply about exactly what level of accountability Singaporeans seek during a particular election cycle.

We have seen the opposition make surges that spark speculation about whether we are on track to a 1.5-party system, only to have the electorate course correct and vote more conservatively in the following election. Clearly, the electorate wants some opposition, but either too much or too little makes the public nervous. As a way to break through this cyclical pattern, the opposition have been trying to sell the idea that voters need to deny the PAP of the super majority of two thirds of parliamentary seats. This would allow the opposition to block constitutional changes. But there is no evidence that this call has been particularly effective.

The second given is that the opposition parties will not form any grand coalition. Minor parties may team up, but big ones won't. At most they will enter into minor pacts to avoid three-cornered fights. I often hear Singaporeans lamenting the fractured state of the opposition. In Malaysia, when former Prime Minister Mahathir Mohamad's Pakatan Harapan coalition ousted Barisan in 2018, some argued that Singapore's opposition would make headway if it were similarly united. These Singaporeans think disunity explains the opposition's lack of success. But this is a fallacy. Opposition disunity is a reflection of voters' own lack of consensus about the kind of political competition they want. Different voters are attracted to different types of opposition.

Therefore, there is no single proven formula for both satisfying hardcore opposition voters, while at the same time, attracting swing voters, first time voters and loyal PAP voters who may be tempted to defect. To put it simply, it is unclear whether the opposition's best bet is to position themselves as a radical alternative to the ruling party, or a sort of PAP-lite.

> In Malaysia, when former Prime Minister Mahathir Mohamad's Pakatan Harapan coalition ousted Barisan in 2018, some argued that Singapore's opposition would make headway if it were similarly united. These Singaporeans think disunity explains the opposition's lack of success. But this is a fallacy. Opposition disunity is a reflection of voters' own lack of consensus about the kind of political competition they want. Different voters are attracted to different types of opposition.

A party that differentiates itself sharply from the PAP by promising free healthcare for example, will no doubt appeal to some voters but will also alienate many others who might see such promises as fiscally irresponsible. On the other hand, a PAP-lite party that only promises changes at the margins, will similarly not be able to please all potential opposition voters. Singaporeans also have different views about the style of politics they want — some prefer their opposition MPs to speak in measured and reasonable tones; others want a bolder, more confrontational approach that shows they will be able to get the better of ministers during parliamentary debates.

This is a dilemma that is not unique to Singapore. The same dynamic is visible in the Democratic Party in the United States and Labour in the United Kingdom. When you are in the opposition, do you move to the centre or do you move further left? We should not underestimate the complexity of this decision, and so we shouldn't be surprised to see opposition parties continue to be divided about the best way forward.

The Workers' Party (WP) is the most successful opposition party of the last 25 years. So perhaps there is something to be said for its controlled and cautious approach — one that infuriates more impatient opposition supporters. Mr Low has been very careful about whom he fields and about

Singapore voters may not have a great appetite for multi-party democracy but they do have an innate sense of fair play.

the causes that he pushes. This is not surprising, seeing that he had a front-row seat witnessing how the PAP demolished his predecessor, the late Mr J.B. Jeyaretnam. Since Mr Low took over, the party has made sure everyone is on message, there are no loose cannons, and they are almost as paranoid of the media as the PAP.

To Mr Low's credit, over the years, he also shared the limelight with Ms Sylvia Lim and Mr Pritam Singh, allowing them to grow in prominence as faces of the WP and, in April 2018, he stepped down as party secretary-general and Mr Singh took over the post. But the WP clearly sees other opposition parties' candidates as potential liabilities to its brand, and thus it will resist forming any coalition.

The Singapore Democratic Party (SDP) traditionally has a bolder and more distinct platform, but its lack of electoral success under Dr Chee Soon Juan has been quite striking since its heyday in 1991. It has consistently performed worse than the opposition average. But it is not clear if this is because of its platform, its style of politicking or a question of personality. It is possible that the PAP did such an effective job of disparaging Dr Chee that his party has been branded unelectable up to now.

Yes, smaller parties are eager to enter into a coalition. Four of them got together recently and they are hoping for Dr Tan Cheng Bock to lead them. It is doubtful that such a coalition would improve these parties' chances.

The third constant is that the opposition will continue to benefit from the underdog advantage. Singapore voters may not have a great appetite for multi-party democracy but they do have an innate sense of fair play. In their own lives, there are enough Singaporeans who feel the system favours privileged elites. So it is not surprising that they identify with candidates who seem to be victims of an overbearing government. The opposition plays the underdog card well and the government seems to know this.

Although it won't create a completely level playing field by allowing electoral boundaries to be set by an independent election commission, for example, it knows it cannot tilt the field to such an extent that elections lose their legitimacy. This was why Prime Minister Lee Hsien Loong said that elections needed to remain contestable and the size of GRCs has shrunk over the past decade, and more Single Member Constituencies (SMCs) have been created to ensure that smaller parties can continue to contest. Thanks to the underdog advantage, voters will give opposition candidates some leeway as long as they do not have disqualifying deficits.

The underdog advantage also means that attacks on the opposition may backfire if they are perceived as over the top. The PAP must be hoping that the government's allegations against the Workers' Party over its handling of its finances will persuade voters that they can't be trusted to run town councils. But it is quite possible that the smears would not just be discounted by the public and instead it will fire up voters to lend their support to a beleaguered opposition. Remember how the WP raised S$1 million in three days through just one online post? This is a sign the PAP cannot ignore.

> The recent string of POFMA interventions may be intended to prove to Singaporeans that opposition viewpoints or opposition facts are hollow. But they could well backfire and add to the perception of unfairness, especially since POFMA only works one way; it cannot be used by opposition politicians to correct false statements made by the PAP government.

Similarly, the recent string of POFMA interventions may be intended to prove to Singaporeans that opposition viewpoints or opposition facts are hollow. But they could well backfire and add to the perception of unfairness, especially since POFMA only works one way; it cannot be used by opposition politicians to correct false statements made by the PAP government.

I would add a caveat though: the underdog advantage doesn't always apply. If the opposition candidate is a non-starter, he is not going to milk any advantage from any PAP attack.

Another very important caveat, as the opposition appear to strengthen, Singaporeans will judge them by higher standards. This could help explain what happened during the 2015 campaign when there was a narrative going around about an impending opposition surge — spread in part by WhatsApp messages about bookies' odds, a subject I will return to later — which resulted in voters being less prepared to give the opposition a break.

THREE UNKNOWNS

On the known unknowns, or the new and less predictable factors in this election, I will cite just three. First, is the question of who really has the upper hand in the online battle for hearts and minds. For a long time, we had assumed that the untamed territory of cyberspace is ruled by opponents of the PAP, but the ruling party and the government were not sitting idly by, especially after the 2011 general election. Government ministers and agencies developed a major official Facebook presence. They have also since been supported by unofficial players, many named and anonymous keyboard warriors and internet brigades. By the 2015 election, these efforts were already significant, as adjunct IPS scholar Tan Tarn How noted, we were seeing "a normalisation of cyberspace"[1]. By this he meant that Singapore's online space was beginning to resemble offline space, that is, largely middle-of-the-road opinions with anti-government voices on the fringe. Just like in the real world, the government's voice was beginning to be among the loudest in the virtual world.

This shift has come about partly because the internet is no longer a minority preoccupation; it is now more reflective of the general public, but it's also because the PAP, like many governments in the world, has embraced the internet and social media.

A very important study done by the Oxford Internet Institute last year, covering 70 countries, found that governments and political parties were engaging in various forms of social media manipulation and disinformation. The methods ranged from using social media to shape public attitudes, to using computational propaganda to suppress human rights, discredit political opponents, and drown out dissenting opinions. Foreign governments have also been known to use similar tools to cause trouble in other polities. The study did not cover Singapore, but it does remind us that internet tools are now at the disposal of all parties, governments included, and of course, as it is not cheap to use these tools at scale, governments with their superior resources can end up the bigger winners. As someone from the media familiar with trying to thrive digitally, being competitive in this space is now big business, data analytics will matter in this election like never before.

---

[1] For the full article, see Tan's "Normalisation of New Media Since the 2011 Election" here: https://ipscommons.sg/normalisation-of-new-media-since-the-2011-election/

The internet has become an arms race; money can make a difference. The 2015 election already gave a hint of how online rumours can sway voters. Remember the so-called bookies' predictions that went viral? A key prediction was that the opposition, the WP in particular, would win at least four GRCs and four SMCs. This could have been bona fide bookies' odds, in which case these bookies are probably out of business; or they could have been attempts to manipulate public opinion. Perhaps, the opposition started these rumours to energise their supporters? Perhaps, the consensus among observers, like political scientist Bilveer Singh, is that the rumours of a big swing towards the opposition helped the PAP. This may have given voters "cold feet" according to Bilveer.

That's 2015. So the big question for 2020 is whether the government's massive investments in online platforms will make this the first election where the internet adds rather than subtracts from the ruling party's already huge offline advantage. It is hard to answer this because we don't even know what is in various parties' online arsenal; we can follow their official accounts but nobody is tracking whether parties can and do micro-target voters, whether or not they are massaging public opinion using trolls or fake accounts, and so on.

But one should also add that the online space remains fundamentally open. Again, as a person from the media, I know that no matter how much resources a dominant organisation may pour into that space, there is only so much they can do to make their content go viral or to stop their opponent's content from going viral. Despite the wealth of data and the science, things can get unpredictable.

The second game changer in this election is the Tan Cheng Bock factor. Major opposition parties have done well to attract credible candidates, including those that the PAP might have also considered to be attractive candidates, but I think it is Tan Cheng Bock's entry into opposition ranks that is ground-breaking. He was no ordinary backbencher; he was a trusted CEC (Central Executive Committee) member. The question is whether he will pave the way for others. I have met a number of Singaporeans who have achieved all they want in their careers and say they now want to contribute to society. They feel Singapore needs to change radically and not just cruise based on what's worked in the past. They are asking themselves: how can I best make a qualitative difference to Singapore? If they are establishment types, it may never have occurred to them to join the opposition -- until now. Will Tan Cheng Bock inspire others to follow in his wake? Of course, much depends on Tan Cheng Bock himself and how he wards off the inevitable verbal blows from the PAP. One big obstacle for him is that many young Singaporeans do not remember his days in Parliament, they know him from the 2011 Presidential Election, and his critics believe he is driven by personal interest and by the conviction that he was robbed of the elected presidency. Dr Tan has cast himself as someone who wants to reclaim the old PAP. The question is whether there are enough people who can tell the difference between the old and the current.

Now, the third uncertainty has to do with how economic and geopolitical conditions will influence voters. In most countries, the state of the economy is the best predictor of elections; the greater the economic turbulence, the more the people are likely to want to vote against the government of the day. In Singapore, it is different. Because of the PAP's status as the natural party of government, Singaporeans have contradictory feelings towards the PAP. When times are bad, they may blame the PAP, and yet they may treat the PAP as a safe haven. This is the inner conflict of many swing voters especially.

It's like how the US dollar paradoxically holds firm or even strengthens when America's problems cause global turbulence. There is a flight to quality in the currency market, so the PAP is like the US dollar of electoral politics, making it quite hard to predict how its value would be affected by economic and geopolitical uncertainty.

On the one hand, the global patterns show voters rejecting establishment politicians in uncertain times, but for the PAP, remember, the biggest ever jump in its vote share occurred in the 2001 election, less than two months after the 9/11 attacks. In the coming election, the opposition may well gain from slower economic growth or voters may heed the PAP call for order and stability at a time of leadership transition.

So I've tried to provide a framework to predict or think about the opposition's chances in the future. Alas, as things stand, we are still trying to peer into a fog — we don't have an election date yet, we don't have the shape of the electoral map, we don't have a good idea of the new faces, and we don't know what the domestic and international environment will be like.

POSTSCRIPT

The Singapore Perspectives conference was held just three days before Singapore had its first COVID-19 case and Hong Kong experienced a surge in infections. Since then, to say the world has not been the same seems like a gross understatement. The coronavirus pandemic has upended lives globally in ways still unfolding.

Since then too, Singapore's political map has changed significantly. The general election of July 10 was held in the midst of the pandemic because the ruling party decided it needed to secure a strong mandate to steer the nation through difficult terrain.

The opposition scored much better than expected, reducing the PAP's vote share from 69.9 per cent to 61.24 per cent and adding another GRC to its side of the ledger, netting a record-breaking 10 seats. It also gave a scare in some constituencies, with former PAP stalwart-turned-opposition-leader Tan Cheng Bock garnering 48.31 per cent of the votes in West Coast GRC, the best performer among the losing teams. Two of his team mates have been inducted as non-constituency MPs.

What about the three stable factors or constants about opposition performance that I cited at the conference? Did these change over the 2020 election? The answer is no. First, indeed they are not and were not a government in waiting and despite the warnings by the ruling party of the prospect of a freak result of the opposition winning the majority of seats, nothing of the sort happened. If anything, the opposition benefited from the exact reverse call. They were not only unable to form the government but there was a very real risk of a wipeout of the opposition, WP Secretary-General Pritam Singh warned voters at the start of the campaign. The plea resonated with swing voters.

Second, as predicted, no grand coalition was formed among the opposition and once again the WP emerged as the pre-eminent party in the camp, garnering all 10 seats but also conducting a campaign on its own terms, voicing out on the eve of polling day an appeal to care for the "intangible aspects" of the country, such as greater openness to other views, culture, creativity, transparency and a free press.

Third, the underdog advantage enjoyed by the opposition held true again as Singaporeans' sense of fair play was affronted by several incidents during the course of the nine-day campaign. Most noteworthy was the attack on a young female candidate on the WP ticket for her allegedly insensitive comments about unequal treatment of minorities. As mentioned in my speech, the government did use POFMA on five occasions during the course of the campaign. Justified or not, these actions fuelled the perception of an unfair contest and that the opposition were being unfairly targeted.

On the known unknowns, I cited the importance of the online space; the Tan Cheng Bock factor and economic and geopolitical conditions. In the end, the pandemic forced nearly all of the campaign to go online, with door-to-door visits severely restricted. As it turned out, the online battle did not give the ruling party a clear advantage, despite its massive resources and surrogates who took on opposition candidates and supporters. Many voters appeared unafraid to make spoofs and memes of ruling party candidates and openly criticised them, using their real names. The so-called climate of fear of possible retribution mattered less to more and more people, it seemed.

PAP Lawrence Wong admitted later that online campaigning did not play to the ruling party's strengths and did not connect with some voters, especially the young. "This was a digital campaign....We tried our best, we produced a lot of good content online. But not all of these connected with netizens...," he said.

Tan Cheng Bock's participation probably contributed to easing the climate of fear as voters saw how even one of its own had turned its back on the ruling party openly. Tan was aided by support from the estranged younger brother of the Prime Minister.

On the impact of prevailing economic and geopolitical conditions on support for the opposition, conventional wisdom had it that in uncertain and troubling times, more voters would opt to stand by the ruling party, as they did in 2001. There was no such swing in 2020. Could this mark the normalisation of Singapore politics, where bad times tend to correlate to poorer outcomes for incumbents like in other systems? The 2020 results form just one data point but, if we exclude the 2015 results, the trend of PAP support holding at around 60 per cent is clear. That threshold may well be in danger of being breached, if the PAP is unable to transform itself and if voters' appetite for greater accountability grows.

CHAPTER 4

Fatalism is Fatal for Small States

BILAHARI KAUSIKAN

Bilateral relations, which I take more generally as international relations, affect Singapore's politics. The most important foreign policy decision we have ever taken was to join Malaysia. It was also the most serious foreign policy miscalculation we have ever made. And in that apparent paradox lies the genesis of independent Singapore's politics. Speaking in the Singapore Legislative Assembly on 5 March 1957, Mr Lee Kuan Yew said, "In the context of the second half of the 20th century, of 20th century Southeast Asia, island nations are a political joke." A political joke. Now, Mr Lee made that statement during a debate on what position to take during the constitutional talks to be held in London. It reflected his conviction, and the conviction of his comrades, that merger with Malaya was the only practical way forward if Singapore were to completely shake off colonial rule.

CONTESTS AND STRUGGLES IN THE 1950s AND 1960s

The political contests of the 1950s and early 1960s that led to merger and then separation, were intertwined with the struggle between left and right, within the Chinese Communist Party-backed United Front, and with the contest against Chinese and Malay chauvinists, in the context of broader global processes of decolonisation and the Cold War. Those experiences shaped our independent political history. To understand Singapore politics, we should juxtapose Mr Lee's 1957 statement with other statements by him and other first-generation leaders describing their experiences in these tangled and incredibly complex processes. Speaking to Mr Dennis Bloodworth — a British journalist — about the PAP's struggles in the communist-supported United Front, Mr Lee said, "Some mug had to do it." Dr Goh Keng Swee echoed the sentiment, "There was really no choice, it was an act of reckless folly. We were five foolish young men and we walked right into it."

Now, Mr Lee's 1957 statement was deterministic. The subsequent statements quoted by Dennis Bloodworth stressed agency and choice, cloaked in self-depreciating irony. As Mr Lee, again quoted by Bloodworth, explained, "We wanted the British out, we believed nationalism to be a more potent force than communism, we pressed on regardless of the horrendous risks."

Our first-generation leaders were practitioners, not theoreticians. But they must have known of Thucydides' too often quoted dictum, "The strong do what they can and the weak suffer what they must." As practitioners, they must have regarded it at best only partially true. Thucydides represents crude realism. Our first-generation leaders were realists, but not crude realists. They understood that crude realism is sometimes not very realistic. There is always agency. Fatalism is fatal. Were it not so, Singapore as we know it today would not exist. Too often, crude realism is just an alibi for unwillingness to take risks, that is to say, to act. There is no action without risk.

Of course, not all risks work out. We all know what happened after merger. And what made it impossible for us to remain in Malaysia ultimately amounted to a point of political philosophy. In the terminology of the day, was it to be a Malaysian Malaysia, or a Malay Malaysia? Our first-generation leadership perhaps underestimated the vehemence with which the Malay leadership in Malaysia clung to the notion of *Ketuanan Melayu* — Malay dominance. Consequently, they underestimated the extent to which their vision of a Malaysian Malaysia based on values we now call multi-racial meritocracy, was unacceptable to the Malaysian Malay leadership. And the fundamental incompatibility of these concepts is still the basic driving force underlying bilateral relations with Malaysia and in a slightly different way, Indonesia too.

AGENCY AS A SMALL STATE

It was not a mistake they would ever make again. Nor should we make the same mistake. But in retrospect, I think it was a happy mistake. Would we have been better off if we had abandoned or fundamentally compromised basic principles in order to remain within Malaysia? Looking at our neighbour today, it is difficult to come to that conclusion. The challenges of those early years were nevertheless very serious, indeed existential. In a book published in 1972, seven years after we were forced out of Malaysia, a British academic by the name of Ian Buchanan predicted, "The future of the city state of Singapore will be largely determined by events in the surrounding countryside of the Malay world, and the Republic can do little more than wait." And he went on to say, "The lines of domestic conflict have already been drawn, Singapore's tragedy is not merely that insurrection will occur in the near future, but that if and when it does occur, it will threaten the very survival of Singapore in Southeast Asia."

Well, needless to say, none of this happened. In truth however, it was often a close-run thing. As Janadas Devan once wrote somewhere, if we made no irretrievable errors, there was certainly a whole lot of trial. But what Buchanan did not understand is how seriously we took multi-racial meritocracy. Having risked an unexpectedly independent Singapore becoming a political joke over this value, we had to make the value work. We certainly did not, as that British academic predicted, "do little more than wait". And so, we are still here.

GLOBAL AND LOCAL CHALLENGES

The Singapore story is the story of the government and people refusing to meekly await their fate, but instead defiantly exercising the agency that is never entirely absent even in the most daunting of circumstances, to ensure that the values for which we risked everything would succeed. That

41

imperative shaped our politics and society. My key point is that there is always agency, there is always something that can be done. Politics, whether of the domestic or foreign variety, is about using the agency that is never entirely absent, even in dire circumstances, to preserve, defend and advance the essential values on which our society is based and which is our unique value proposition. We cannot be just like everybody else. If a small country is just like every other country, it risks becoming irrelevant; a political joke.

I think we have entered an era in which our unique method of organising politics and society; our unique value proposition — and don't forget, it is unique because in that enormous region we now call the Indo-Pacific, every other country, without exception, organises politics and society on the basis of a formal or informal ethnic or religious hierarchy — is going to be assailed by an array of powerful global forces that will seriously test that value proposition.

Technologies of various kinds are forcing disruptive changes at a historically unprecedented pace. And this is weakening the sense of national identity and cohesion, on which all politics must be based. Powerful centrifugal forces have been set in motion. This has caused transnational and subnational identities of various kinds to be aggressively asserted everywhere. And all this is occurring at a time when geopolitics is in a more than usual state of flux, and some major powers do not hesitate to try to harness identities for their own ends. I see no reason why Singapore should be somehow magically exempted from these global trends.

Identity politics is already upon us, although usually not overtly labelled identity politics. For example, lurking within debates about the role of foreigners in our economy is really a claim of hierarchy based on a different set of values, and such claims are far too often not uncontaminated, much as those who make them may deny it, by claims of ethnic privilege. That is only one example. A moment's thought will bring others to mind. We are going to hear much more about all these issues when the next general election gets under way.

At the same time, I sense that, perhaps unsettled by the vast, impersonal, and only dimly comprehended, global forces that are swirling all around us, some Singaporeans feel deeply insecure in the face of a future that can be only glimpsed as through a glass, darkly. I hope I am wrong, but that is what

> In broad outline, the essential problems that we now face are enhanced 21st century iterations of issues that we have faced down before. We were able to do so because our first-generation leaders were a rare mixture, a rare blend of political skill and technocratic competence. That is why Singapore succeeded when so many other countries that gained independence around the same time, floundered in the face of similar challenges. As Singapore prospered, politics receded. But we are now entering a period, and I think it will be a lengthy period, when leadership will again require a melding of political skill and technocratic competence. And so, the lessons of our early political history are more relevant than ever and need to be re-emphasised.

I sense. And this could make us vulnerable to external and internal snake oil salesmen peddling simplistic solutions.

How do we deal with this? In broad outline, the essential problems that we now face are enhanced 21st century iterations of issues that we have faced down before. We were able to do so because our first-generation leaders were a rare mixture, a rare blend of political skill and technocratic competence. That is why Singapore succeeded when so many other countries that gained independence around the same time, floundered in the face of similar challenges. As Singapore prospered, politics receded. But we are now entering a period, and I think it will be a lengthy period, when leadership will again require a melding of political skill and technocratic competence. And so, the lessons of our early political history are more relevant than ever and need to be re-emphasised.

II

New Forms and Movements

Introductory Remarks

FARISH A. NOOR

This was an exciting forum on new forms and movements in society. In this day and age, many of us are familiar with the themes that have been in circulation in the media for decades. Today we talk about the age of disruption, and there has been a lot of talk about the possible end of the nation state, how globalisation has created all kinds of new communicative infrastructures, bringing about new social movements.

But despite all this talk that has actually gone on from the 1980s to the 1990s, the nation state is still the dominant actor in international relations and we see that the nation state has not lost its relevance in politics, both domestically and internationally. However, we cannot deny the fact that in practically every society in the world today, we are looking at social landscapes and political landscapes that are very different. And one major reason for this is the prominence of new actors on the landscape, on the stage of national politics.

When we look at human history, we can see that practically every good idea that has brought out positive social change and progress has been criticised at the outset, and this is not something unique in Asia or in Singapore. A hundred years ago, it was deemed perfectly all right to send children to work in factories or send them down the coal mine, because of the prevailing view that children had no rights. Someone had to come up with the idea that children are human beings endowed with rights, and then advocate for that for there to be a change in society's attitude. Changes such as these were often initiated by those we would call outliers, those who were outside the system.

So when we talk about change, we need to recognise that change can often be difficult, and this is how we challenge opinions. Most of us here have witnessed change in the course of our lives. We see it all the time, happening around us in many ways. Even our understanding of humour has changed over the years. I am not sure how many of you here remember the comedy programme called *The Benny Hill Show*, that was once popular up to the 1970s and 1980s. Such humour was once deemed popular, but no longer. We don't find the show, with its sexist and degrading jokes, funny in any way. Why? It's not because the jokes have changed, it's because society has changed — and for the right reasons.

When these changes happen, they often involve people advocating for a different way of looking at this. Understanding that climate issues are common concerns, understanding that migrant workers are fellow human beings, understanding that underprivileged women are human beings who deserve a chance. Someone has to advocate for that. This section looks precisely at these sorts of groups that are emerging in Singapore today, symptomatic with what is happening worldwide.

A/Prof Crystal Abidin is Principal Research Fellow in the Faculty of Humanities, Curtin University, and she will discuss the emergence of newer forms of digital activism. Mr Cai Yinzhou has been working on the ground with different social groups and is Director of Citizen Adventures. Ms Carrie Tan, Founder and Strategic Advisor of Daughters of Tomorrow, has been working with and advocating for women for many years. Finally, Ms Nor Lastrina Hamid, Co-founder of Singapore Youth for Climate Action, will speak about the climate movement in Singapore. The themes of their own work as you can tell are very pertinent to the needs and concerns of the age that we live in.

CHAPTER 5

Activism in Singapore in the Digital Age: Influencer Cultures, Meme Factories, and Networked Virality

CRYSTAL ABIDIN

I'm a Principal Research Fellow of internet studies and I'm an anthropologist by training. What this means is I spend a lot of time looking at what young people — especially in Singapore but also in the Asia Pacific — do on the internet. I don't mean I just sit behind a computer and look at them online, I also spend extensive periods with these young people in different domains — where they live, where they work, in order to find out what they do online, and what it means for them.

My research typically consists of things in the Singapore context, like influencers, internet celebrities, meme cultures, viral videos, so on and so forth. I hope to also highlight a few things about social media and network cultures in Singapore in today's climate.

THE SINGAPORE CONTEXT

First off, as all good academics do, here's a bit of context. The Singapore context is a little bit different from the rest of Southeast Asia. First, we have to consider the structure. We have a normative state surveillance culture in which we believe that if the state is watching us through those scary "spiderweb-like" cameras at the MRT stations or along the streets at night, we tend to believe that this is for our protection and for our wellbeing. There is also a very high level of tacit IT knowledge among our citizens; you look at kindergarteners, kids in primary schools — they are already learning how to use technology, IT and devices, and it's systemic throughout all levels of society.

Secondly, moving on to culture, we also have a situation of media didacticism. What this means is if you turn on a Jack Neo movie or a Channel 8 TV series at prime time, chances are every single episode or movie is going to be delivering some sort of moral message, on how to be a better Singaporean or a better person in life. But in tandem with this, we also have the culture of public shaming that is a result of an institution known as STOMP. Now, for a long time, STOMP has been a cornerstone of internet culture in Singapore, where every day ordinary citizens get to upload or display online anything that they feel is pertinent to their concerns. This can be a reckless driver on the streets, or an National Service man in uniform who's supposedly not allowed take a seat in an empty train cabin because they are meant to be vigilant and to protect their country at all times.

Finally, we also have the third pillar, looking at agency. Singapore is a relatively small country in terms of land size, but we are very dense. This lends us to feelings of anomie where it's easy to feel invisible, nameless and faceless in the crowd. Yet, at the same time, with the added factor of lateral surveillance from public cameras, the idea that at any time any citizen can come and "STOMP" you also makes citizens feel that while being faceless and nameless, they might also be watched.

What I do in this context of Singapore is to study how internet pop culture relates to everyday life and identity politics. Today, I want to surface three topics from my research, and the impact they have on Singapore society.

INFLUENCER CULTURES

Let's look at two examples of influencer culture in Singapore. Influencers in Singapore, for the most part, tend to be degraded; they tend not to be spoken of very kindly. It is not uncommon to have Singaporeans accuse them of being "attention seekers", just out here to grab your attention online and then sell you something via a "#sponsored" post. But if you were to go back to the very early beginnings of influencer culture in Singapore, from 2005, a lot of these personalities originated from grassroots groups, young people on the fringes, or minority race, sexuality or gendered groups, who had messages that they wanted to share with young people in society.

My favourite example is the YouTube Malay and Arab duo, known as MunahHirziOfficial. Now, some of you may remember that across all their parody videos, this particular one from 2016 stood out. A Malay woman had submitted an application form in order to put up a pop-up stall in a mall in the eastern part of Singapore. But her application was denied because the mall "was trying to cater to a Chinese audience". And this Malay woman did not want to stomach this "feedback" without a fight. That story came out in a string of news articles, but it was very quickly buried. What soon happened was that influencers like MunahHirziOfficial took that incident as their inspiration, and produced parody videos to show what it's like to "reverse" this discriminatory situation. One video was about them in a Malay-dominated nightclub declining an application form from a Chinese *ah lian* wanting to hold a birthday party in the club, because they do not want to "cater" to the majority race in this parody situation.

If you were a "woke" Singaporean — as young people say these days — you will understand this context exactly. It is parody meant to push forth messages of anti-racism. But if say, you were just a regular Beyoncé, Nicki Minaj, Ariana Grande fan and you know of these "vehicles", you know of these pop songs that go viral nationally and internationally, then this may come across to you as just another local parody. The implication of the political message may be lost on you, but you still get a semblance that parody is a strong vehicle for people in the margins and in the fringes to share messages to the mainstream in a palatable way, via humour.

A more recent case in point is the Nair siblings: musician Subhas and influencer Preeti. They produced a parody video to highlight the racism that they had observed in a "brownface" incident that occurred in our country.

We also want to look at influencers who are amplifying messages to do with gender and sexuality. Again, my favourite example, MunahHirziOfficial presented trans people, intersex people, people who are fluid on the gender spectrum, unapologetically occupying space in public, in a parody music video — as resistance through pop culture. But we also have the more traditional, "old school" influencers and bloggers — as we used to call them from 2005 — who used to put up provocative content, at first to shock and scare people, but eventually to deliver a "#sponsored" message, once again.

Case in point: the lifestyle blogger, Holly Jean, who for a stretch of days went very silent on the internet after a supposed viral video of her engaging in an intimate act was posted. Shortly after that, in the days that passed, she eventually released an extended video showing that this was all part of a campaign from Durex to teach young people that even in a moment of heat, in a moment of passion, there's always time to put on a condom. So, we see influencers using very creative ways to promote conversation around issues that are difficult to talk about in mainstream society, in formats that are more palatable and interesting to the young people they have to reach.

MEME FACTORIES

The second type of research that I do looks at the idea of "meme factories". Meme factories generally contribute to the normalisation of ideas. They make permissible what people may feel afraid to discuss openly in everyday conversation, and they also give young people a vocabulary for talking about things that may be contentious.

Back in about 2015, Member of Parliament Mr Baey Yam Keng posted a tribute in the wake of the Paris attacks. He posted a very sincere caption with a picture of himself last taken at the Eiffel Tower. On Facebook though, young citizens — or as we call them in Singapore, young netizens — took to memeing him, and photoshopping him next to many different monuments to articulate that they felt the aesthetic of his picture was not palatable. Here, memeing served as a form of critique and criticism, albeit clouded in humour. And this was an instantaneous way to get feedback from the ground, "live" as things unfolded.

These days, we also have different types of meme factories perpetuating on Instagram. Two of my favourites are Kiasu Memes for Singaporean Teens, and highnunchicken. In 2019, some memes were created to reference a series of sexual assaults cases that came to light at the National University of Singapore in that year. At first, this issue surfaced because an under-graduate, Monica Baey took to Instagram to share her experiences, before it got widely taken up by other influencers, other prominent young people who use social media, and indeed other people who run meme factories, in order to normalise the conversation. It is not that they were trying to normalise the criminal act, but they were equipping young people with vocabulary —

whether through humour, through parody, through critique, through the language of social justice — to talk about these issues openly.

NETWORKED VIRALITY

The third thread of my research looks at networked threads and virality. Groups may coagulate and congregate online, on social media pages, groups or forums. Earlier, I mentioned the Preeti and Subhas Nair satirical video, calling out the Nets e-pay brownface advertisement. That incident was initially publicised by the editor-in-chief of *Mynah* magazine, Ruby Thiagarajan in a Twitter thread. Likewise, Monica Baey who initiated a whole national conversation about sexual harassment and "#MeToo", first sparked it off in a series of Instagram posts.

But long before social media was adopted by these very young millennials and Gen Zs, we had the good old SMRT Ltd (Feedback). For those of us who still use Facebook — probably millennials and older — and for those of us who still remember what SMRT Ltd (Feedback) used to do, we will recall that they were a network of people who were very involved in tech, who were sometimes called "online trolls", who were sometimes called a "meme group". At the height of their activity, a lot of people were submitting to them instances of what they felt were injustices befalling fellow citizens.

Case in point: a tourist who had been scammed and conned by people who operated mobile phone services in Sim Lim Square, despite going viral on social media, did not yet receive proper legal or police redress for their complaints. So SMRT Ltd (Feedback) and a group of very enthusiastic citizens came together to name and shame some of the people who ran the scams. But they also came together to organise relief efforts, fundraising efforts, in order to help chase down these errant shopkeepers and to help their victims.

PITFALLS

As much as this seems very optimistic, and that it feels really good to tell you about all the wonderful things that very young people are doing on the internet, there are also some pitfalls. If you were to look at influencers who primarily serve as amplification platforms, it's great that they are giving us the vocabulary and a sense of urgency to talk about race, gender, sexuality, and the like. But you must also remember that these tend to be minority influencers, influencers from civil society who sometimes may not always be able to prioritise their rice bowls. They are engaging in such work with very little support and sustenance.

Further, if we were to look at some of the most popular YouTube channels and networks in Singapore that are predominantly run by Chinese youth, you often see that they use minority or fringe identities as a punchline. You see men who dress effeminately in skits, and who use derogatory terms about trans peoples. You see Chinese YouTubers who caricature the minority races in their skits, and play on stereotypes like "Indian men are to be feared" and "Malays are lazy". On the surface, this may seem like comedy. These things go under the radar; we don't discuss them, we don't call them out to the same extent as we do many other incidents, because they feel "normal", they feel "common", and the jokes have been mainstreamed and normalised by everyday society. Influencers can sometimes also perpetuate these harms.

In the same way, the meme factories that have been helping to normalise difficult conversations also have pitfalls. Zuraidah had earlier mentioned [in her talk] the notion of the "internet brigade" — sometimes when we see all these consolidated and networked posts online, especially on Facebook, many of them are actually artfully architectured by groups of people who push out the same message at the same time under the guise that this is an "organic" grassroots sentiment. We now know from research all throughout Southeast Asia that these are architects of misinformation, disinformation, and attention hacking. We now also know that they are for hire, whether pro-state, anti-state, or even just to sponsor or elevate sponsored products for all sorts of corporate clients. So as we celebrate meme factories and the joy they bring us on the internet from their humour, we also want to think about the sources, the agenda, and who's channelling all of these contents to us.

Lastly, the pitfalls of networked threads: While they do a very good job in surfacing issues that normally fly under the radar, we also have to be aware of mob mentality. I work and live in Perth in Western Australia. In the last seven to eight years, many people who have been named and shamed by STOMP and by the wider internet mob in Singapore have fled to Perth. They have gone there to seek refuge, because they feel that out here on the streets in Singapore they may be hounded by Singaporeans, or risk being called out in person. This is something that we have to address, and something that reminds us of the power, the transferability, and the online-offline "bleeding" capacity of internet culture, with consequences on everyday life.

At the same time, we don't want to plainly discard these efforts as just "Millennials doing a woke thing online" or "Gen Z wanting to be very politically correct". Because the last thing we want is for our young people to have "call out" fatigue, to have feelings of invisibility and abandonment, as if they are unable to participate in society, because nobody listens to them.

Do not belittle the format. As much as it comes across as funny, frivolous, and humorous, it is designed to be relatable and to reach audiences beyond our imagination.

I want to end with two quick points. What should we make of everyday politics and internet pop culture? The first: do not belittle the format. As much as it comes across as funny, frivolous, and humorous, it is designed to be relatable and to reach audiences beyond our imagination. And finally: don't underestimate the authority of where these sources come from. They may not

Don't underestimate the authority of where these sources come from. They may not always seem like the most learned or most certified people, but the networks of their power and information circuits are extremely dispersed, and when they consolidate, that's when you really see the subversive power of them all.

always seem like the most learned or most certified people, but the networks of their power and information circuits are extremely dispersed, and when they consolidate, that's when you really see the subversive power of them all.

6

Lorongs of Wisdom

CAI YINZHOU

I would like to thank IPS for this opportunity be alongside stellar allies in the space of social advocacy. To be selected from a huge pool of existing thought leaders on different causes and representations is indeed an honour. Most of my work is geographically specific to two neighbourhoods, Geylang and Dakota Crescent. Geylang being the place I grew up and Dakota Crescent an adjacent neighbourhood where my grandma had lived. These are the two locations where I have spent most of my life and where I draw reference from.

I've named the talk today, "Lorongs of Wisdom", in light of my journey to advocacy and the attribution of the close association of identity with the stereotypes of the neighbourhood I was born in.

CHANGING LANDSCAPES OF MY HOME, GEYLANG

Most people know Geylang for different reasons. However, growing up having to constantly debunk such perspectives about a place I called home was quite unnerving, to least to say. But from the state's perspective, there was also some truth contained in this stereotype. Crime rates and vice there were extremely high. A former police commissioner once described it as a "keg of gunpowder ready to explode". However, in order to understand the context of vice activities solidifying in Geylang, we have to trace the historical pathways of these activities as well.

It all started in 1819 when Singapore was established as a free-trading port. Being a free-trading port, the government did not tax trade and had to look for other revenue means. One of these was through implementing of taxation and licenses to vices that were already happening here. In 1820, you can open a gambling farm for $95 per month.

In the 1830s, the opium regulation allowed the sale of opium, together with tobacco and alcohol, which were also highly taxable vices. In the 1860s there was a huge influx of migrants, mostly young unmarried males who tipped the gender imbalance to 14 males to 1 female. In order to maintain social order, prostitution was then legalised. Sex work by mostly foreign women was tolerated and happened in designated brothels. All these didn't happen in Geylang just yet, it was all concentrated at the Singapore River.

After self-governance in 1959, there was a concerted effort to eradicate organised crime groups, many of whom were managing these vices. The Land Acquisition Act in 1967 resettled many of these areas, moving them to the city fringes and beyond. So, just a fun historical fact, for some of you who may not know, in 1915, there were three junk ships that were anchored off Changi Point, Pulau Ubin and Pasir Panjang. For $5 you could be taken on board for a whole day at sea inclusive of food and a girl thrown in. This is the historical context and with the multiple clampdowns and eventual designation of these activities in Geylang as a red-light district, thus consolidating the vices there.

People often ask me, why doesn't the government shut everything down. A similar question in Parliament in 1999 led the Minister of Home Affairs then to explain that it's better to know where they are rather than to disperse them and send them underground. So the policy of containment and control was indeed a pragmatic approach dealing with such vices and prostitution.

As such, Geylang's reputation is actually an urban planning decision. An allocation as a sacrificial lamb for the rest of Singapore to be "safe". So what does it mean then for me growing up there in ground zero of this containment zone?

I have witnessed first-hand the constant tension between the state and these vices. Eventually, my lived experiences are encompassed by many encounters within.

THE BACKALLEY BARBER: DOING RIGHT
BY MY FOREIGN FRIENDS

One encounter was with a population of people. Statistically they are about one-fifth of our population, many of them live in Geylang and are males.

They are our low-wage migrant workers. They mostly work in construction. Some of them do the jobs that we wouldn't aspire to, like cleaning, construction and marine, but for which we are quite completely dependent on. Although there are purpose-built dormitories, many of them who live in places like Geylang and Little India. They are attracted to these places by cheap rent, and normally live in the dilapidated shophouses and old apartments. Unfortunately, many of them have been found to live in quite squalid conditions, and here was where I met the first group of friends in Geylang from Bangladesh.

They were all young men and we gathered to play badminton on weekend evenings in 2013. Many of them shared what they have given up to come here and I was very inspired as a youth. Although we were similar in age, the sacrifices they made were on a completely different level from the decisions that I have to make as a Singaporean. Interacting with them on a level of friendship really changed the labels I associated them with — as migrant workers. Though I was told by my parents that migrant workers were dangerous, one such personal encounter changed that altogether.

This is Bashar, he's from Bangladesh and came to Singapore with his twin brother when they were just 22. They actually left medical school back home to work here because their father had a stroke. In order to feed their family, Bashar worked as an electrician. At that point of time when I met him, he hadn't cut his hair for six months, and being a friend, the least I could do was learn how to cut hair on YouTube and give him a haircut. I could've actually just paid for a haircut but I chose to do that because that's what friends do. Both of us were quite poor then, anyway.

Bashar was the first of many migrant workers that I eventually cut hair for. The sole purpose wasn't to do charity, neither was it done out of pity for them — but really because of the impactful conversations I had with them where many shared stories of sacrifice, of what they had to give up just to come to Singapore to work. In turn, giving the prime years of their lives to us. So what are some possibilities or solutions within these communities if we dare to imagine? It starts when we really talk to these populations instead of just talking about them.

We started to organise events and activities from 2013 in the back alleys and in dormitories, inviting Singaporeans to have their perception changed through interactions with migrant workers over food and activities. In 2015, we started tours after some participants of these events reflected on their fascination with the neighbourhood. For us, it was an opportunity to rethink this area as a social ecosystem with different groups of people interdependent on one another, and to speak beyond the labels of vice that we know of Geylang to be — to a perspective that is alive, interdependent on not just one another in Geylang but with the rest of us in Singapore.

SPREADING LOVE TO OTHER HOMES: DAKOTA CRESCENT AND BEYOND

I transferred this methodology of doing tours to Dakota Crescent in 2015 when it was announced that Dakota Crescent would expire by 2016. It was actually a neighbourhood that my Grandma grew up in and lived at towards her last few years, and I was extremely close to her. In my interactions with the residents at Dakota Crescent, I realised that many of them had their own stories to tell. But being elderly and from a rental flat community, they didn't have much of a platform where they were empowered to speak. So I organised a group of them and as a tour guide, we worked together to create a tour that we could bring Singaporeans on. Except it was quite different experience, not so much talking about the built architecture or nostalgic merits of the place for which it was publicised during SG50, but really about the people and the place, and the connections that they had.

Many of you in the room probably lived through that time period of resettlement and relocation as well. The residents who took on the role of tour guides did too, not just showing participants around their neighbourhood, but also showing many of the Singaporeans who came, how life was like for them as a community. This led to us eventually not just conducting tours, but embarking on a multimedia documentation project online on betweentwohomes.sg, as well as a conservation report documenting the merits of the place from the people's perspective. Eventually this led to a partial conservation of the blocks. However, with the residents moving, the reality of relocation was still a problem. Many of such issues that they faced were also met with spontaneous solutions that were led by the needs that the residents have.

Together with friends and families, we rallied around together to help the residents move to the new estates. Rebuilding the relationships that they had lost with their neighbours and also connecting them in a very urban HDB setting that was different from the quaint, spread out design that the Dakota Crescent SIT flats had. For years, rental flat communities have been designed and built in their own silos and I'm glad to see efforts of reversing all these through social mixing.

What exactly do we do at Citizen Adventures? What we really want to do is to build bridges and not walls. And also look at how we as citizens can find the good in everybody, to love our neighbours, and to resist the systemic labels placed on these populations through friendships and create new norms.

The rental flat design is also similar to how we design recreation centres and migrant worker dormitories. These had been called social ghettos and as I said, I'm glad to see it being reversed through

> We look to these social issues as not just issues in their own silo, but as mirrors which reflect the values of our society.

new designs of blocks that are mix of rental and purchase, but also even in schools where we are encouraging mixing of students of different races and socio-economic strata. So back to the point of social norms, the question is always, what kind of norms do we want to create as citizens. As people who care, how do we get people to also know about these norms? And allow these new norms to sit well within our population?

And it first has to start from ourselves. So we need new role models to exemplify the values that we want to see in our society. From a three-year old child to Members Parliament of various constituencies who value the efforts of those who keep our estates clean, whether local or foreigners, or to the ordinary Singaporeans who open up their hearts by opening up their homes, we look to these social issues as not just issues in their own silo, but as mirrors which reflect the values of our society.

SEEING THEM AS PEOPLE, NOT STATS

Clans and associations is the last point that I would like to make. Immigrants, many of them who came in early Singapore formed these organisations as mutual self-help groups to support one another in a faraway land, not just focusing on developing their own villages back home, but also eventually contributing to much of public infrastructure by building our first schools, hospitals in Singapore. Although many of the low-wage migrant workers back then were doing hard labour, there was a dignity in the process of gathering and seeing a sliver of hope as they found community here.

And this is one of the dreams that we have for these groups of migrant workers that we hang out with, now called Singapore Migrant Friends (SMF). Every Sunday they play volleyball at Kallang field. They are one of the many self-organised migrant groups there. SMF consists of four different nationalities apart from Singaporeans who gather every week to hang out with them, have food and play volleyball. Apart from engaging migrant workers as statistics that we see in our midst, we could also see them as people.

My initiative, BackAlley Barbers, was featured in during the National Parade 2018. It was heartening to see many Singaporeans rallying around the need to care for people around us in our midst as well.

I even went to Bangladesh to visit Bashar at his house when he got married where I got a haircut from his barber as well. BackAlley Barbers has grown to a team of 42 barbers, we are all skills-based, long-term volunteers that go around giving free haircuts in migrant shelters, nursing homes and rental flat communities. We are also building an employability programme to recruit and employ people with special needs, as well as planning to start our own barber shop. All this is really about identifying these issues not just as issues, but as social ecosystems.

So the dream is really to move beyond the economic, but also the social and environmental perceptions that we have, and also to find the non-Googleables in our neighbourhoods through the conversations that we have had — whether amongst our friends, in schools or workplaces to see communities as social ecosystem independent, interdependent on one another. And starting from humanising the narrative, to find strength and diversity and perhaps beyond the labels that we put on one another — to talk *to* one another, and stop talking *about* one another.

7

Removing Barriers, Excavating Potential from the Underserved

CARRIE TAN

I would really like to extend my very sincere thanks to IPS for having me as well as my peers in the civil society space share about our work. This platform is so invaluable for those of us who are seeking to inform and potentially influence policies through the work we do on the ground in our communities. Dr Lam talked about whether there's a possibility that politics in Singapore would shift from a politics of survival to a politics of aspiration. Personally, I would like to think that this is the beginning. Having us on this panel precisely is about politics and aspiration put into action!

I do not presume that many of you would know about Daughters of Tomorrow's (DOT) work. So I would like to share a little bit. We don't have the time to go into the breadth and the depth of everything DOT does, but I hope that with this overview and summary, you can get a bit of context of how our work actually is, well, kind of political in a way but also not quite.

HELPING "UNHELPABLE" WOMEN

To give a brief background about the women that we work with, these are the demographics. They belong to the bottom 10% of Singapore's socio-economic class — of whom 80% have secondary school or lower education; 40% are single mothers; 80% are from ethnic minority groups; and about a fifth of them are migrant mothers on long-term visit passes. So they range from having two to nine children, and the women who come through our doors range from those in their 20s to their 50s and 60s. And their

> I learnt that poverty was actually an issue beyond just finances. And that it depletes people in many ways beyond that.

households all earn less than $650 per capita per month, which qualifies them for the ComCare financial assistance.

I would like to take a moment to invite you, to try and imagine or think about these statistics and your impression of this group of women. I think the predominant narrative today often describes these women as being people in need, or needy, disadvantaged or vulnerable — and on the most positive end of that scale, we see them as very resilient amidst their struggles. I would like to invite you to hold onto these impressions as I continue with my presentation.

To go back, in 2014 when I first seeded the idea and wanted to start this organisation, I actually approached a specialist agency whose mission was to help mothers return to the workforce. The conversation with them was enlightening, but also quite disappointing and frustrating at that time. I spoke to them about whether they were helping these women at the bottom of the pyramid. And their response to me was that they found it very difficult to help them and they expressed disbelief that I would actually try to or attempt to help this group. Adding to this, the agency felt that these women did not seem like they wanted to help themselves, making it even more challenging. So I made the conclusion at that point in time that somehow this community of women were dismissed or perhaps reluctantly relegated to "unhelpable", or to use a politically incorrect phrase, "cannot make it".

So over the next six years, I set up DOT and we went about discovering many things about the women — and since 2015, we have rendered support to more than 1,000 women from the low-income community. Since 2018 we have managed to put a 140 of them back into the workforce. This may not look like a statistically very impressive number but I think in view of the barriers that they are facing or they had faced, it is quite a promising figure.

CORRECTING THE MYTH OF POVERTY BEING ONLY ABOUT DOLLARS AND CENTS

Some of the lessons learnt when working with this community were very shocking to me and also very useful in helping us to formulate our programmes. I learnt that poverty was actually an issue beyond just finances. And that it depletes people in many ways beyond that.

The first thing I realised — as to why women were not coming to attend programmes by various workforce agencies — was that they didn't even have enough money to pay for bus fares. The other thing was that they could have wanted to come to the workshops, but looking at the statistics, of how many children they have, and the fact that half of them are single mothers, they really lack the family support or other kinds of childcare support to allow them to actually attend any kind of skills upgrading or employability programmes. We also noticed that amongst the women that we served, at least 25 or 27 per cent of them suffered from some form of mental health problems, such as anxiety and depression, and uniformly all of them suffered from low self-confidence or self-esteem.

So we started off with my team being a charity, and then we extended our partnerships with a lot of private companies who do CSR with us. We formulated a process or journey to help improve the women's confidence while providing them with moral support and emotional support through volunteer befrienders. We also went all the way through soft skills training to skills training, or bridging them to vocational training to even linking them with employers that are sensitised by us on the challenges of those who work or live with very scarce resources, especially financial resources. The extra mile that we went to in terms of helping these "unhelpable" community was in providing for every single workshop that we run, until today, childminding provisions, which means that we will have the women attend class in one room and have a separate room for them to bring their kids, and we have volunteers roped in from various sources to help mind the children while the mothers learn in peace.

So this is the array of work that we do on a programmatic level, but we are also very proud to share that we have in some ways contributed to certain key advocacy wins such as the debarment rule for housing for single parents. We work very closely with AWARE and Member of Parliament Louis Ng on this issue — of whether single mothers or single parents could buy housing — when we realised that a lot of housing instability contributed to the women's stresses and that they weren't able to settle down and be able to commit to a job when they were having housing instability.

The other advocacy win that we had recently was when the Ministry of Social and Family Development (MSF) announced that childcare subsidies that used to only cater to women in employment was now extended to women who were looking for employment. Although we never got a very definite acknowledgement that it was us who pushed for and succeeded in this advocacy, I think we spent a good part of 2014 to 2017, talking to anybody who would listen to us, whether they were social workers, or social service agencies, or social service officers, anybody we met from MSF about how women were not able to come to class, etc., because they didn't have childcare provisions. So we were quite happy that this kind of, well, subtle complaining or highlighting of issues to policymakers actually helped in enhancing some policies.

In the private sector, too, we saw that there was a very strange gap between the needs for workforce and actual successes in hiring. We saw that a lot of the sectors in Singapore, like F&B, retail and hospitality, were always looking to hire locals, but they didn't seem to be getting much headway; yet we have on the other hand a pool of 25,000 local women looking for employment. After really working alongside employers and the women for several years, we correctly diagnosed that the main barrier was that these sectors traditionally structure their work in a kind of shift work or rostered schedules. This means that an employee would potentially be rotated up to three different shifts in a week — and for a single mother who is not able to afford a domestic helper and could only rely on the standard 7am to 7pm childcare, there is no way they could have been able to take up positions in these jobs that sometimes require them to work night shifts.

So we set about advocating for what we call core and stable scheduling to private sectors employers and explaining to them that these women want work, they are willing to work hard, but the only thing they need accommodation with is that they be given office hours for non-office jobs so that they can pick up their kids in childcare by 7pm. Since we started this advocacy in September 2018, the first three months yielded around 30 companies coming on board to offer core and stable scheduling, and I'm very happy to share an updated figure that by December 2019, the total number of companies that have pledged and offer core and stable schedule to women in the workplace is now 96, and across many different sectors that the women were previously unable to access.

THE WOMEN OF DOT

I am proud of the wonderful team at DOT and the inspiring women we serve. I would like to share some notable examples of women we have helped. An example of a success story is Dalina. She was offered core and stable scheduling with a local employer The Coconut Club. The job helped her juggle caregiving needs of her elderly mother. Another success story is Norlia. She benefited from a programme we pioneered called the Eldercare Program. It is for low-income women to take up positions as healthcare assistants in elderly homes. The nursing homes as well as daycare centres continue to have high demand for labour, but are right now still very much dependent on foreign workforce. I'm quite happy to share that there have been many success cases of local women entering these eldercare sectors in the past two years. As for Norlia, she has been promoted recently and she is mentoring other DOT women who have entered the same institution she's in, which is Vanguard Healthcare's Pearl's Hill Care Home.

Coming back to the impressions of these women at the beginning of this presentation — whether they are needy, vulnerable or disadvantaged — I would like to share about Zarina who is one of our beneficiaries as well as our community leader in our Women in Action Community Childminding Network. In October 2019, Zarina shared her community leadership experience with 70 social workers and students at the National University of Singapore, and this was facilitated by one of our colleagues, herself was a former social worker. We were very heartened that Zarina was able to bring her perspective into a room full of social workers and students who were aspiring to become social workers — to share about her experiences and role in the community as a facilitator between women who needed childminding services and those who were able to provide child minding services from their homes.

Other proud examples include Siti and Rozie. At the 2019 Asian Venture Philanthropy Network's conference, they talked about their community-organising experience with impact investors from the global community. I'm just really proud that we are able to put women's voices on big platforms. We have gone beyond just representing them — to talk about them such as what I'm doing today and even have them at the table for important discussions

An individual's potential is often limited by society's perception of them.

pertaining to investments and funding for the work that they do and we do with them at the community level.

Being the social activist that I am, I would like to encourage everyone to be inspired by the stories of the successes of the women that I have shared, that truly an individual's potential is often limited by society's perception of them. And I think as a community and as policy makers, I encourage you to think about the low-income community not just as needy or deserving only of financial aid — but also of financial investment to help them fulfil their potential and to help them in social mobility.

POSTSCRIPT: REFLECTING ON THE COVID-19 PANDEMIC

To say a lot has happened since Singapore Perspectives 2020 in January is an understatement. From a global pandemic the likes of which none in our generation has ever experienced to the general election (GE) and me becoming a Member of Parliament. — COVID-19 has put a spotlight on the struggles of the vulnerable in society, for whom I am grateful to now have a larger platform to serve and enable.

The pandemic has really thrown up a situation where more and more in society are going to be impacted by the ensuing economic recession. We don't know what the economy is going to look like, and when it is going to recover. All along, within our thinking about social services and social assistance, there has been this unconscious narrative of who are the "deserving" people in society that should be helped. Our meritocratic system also created an unfortunate side effect of unconscious judgments about those who need state assistance, as somehow not "good enough", or not trying hard enough for themselves.

My wish and work will be for people to develop more empathy for one another through the common experience of struggle. Because so many more people will fall into hard times, not for lack of trying or effort on their part, but simply due to the challenges and circumstances of the time. I hope that the word "deserving" can be removed from our national vocabulary when thinking about social assistance. Instead of being cumbersome, mammoth structures that are hard to navigate, policies need to be considered and implemented accessibly, with the key priority of lifting the human spirit, especially in such challenging times.

The recent GE has shown that some Singaporeans are keen to see more openness in the way sensitive topics like race and discrimination are discussed. When we start talking about those topics, it is important that we go beyond rhetoric, narratives and ideology, to delve further into the experience and sentiments of those marginalised and their lived realities. Together with my esteemed colleagues, I hope to facilitate conversations within and outside Parliament that foster greater empathy and understanding, in turn producing more inclusive policies to improve lives.

My wish is for Singapore, and our policies to reflect and extend graciousness, generosity and kindness in providing assistance, access and equity to those who need them, with no judgment. Through this, we will enable the uplifting of our people's spirit, and together, forge a kinder and more resilient citizenry to emerge stronger from the crisis.

CHAPTER 8

Creating and Uniting a Climate-Conscious Singapore

NOR LASTRINA HAMID

Thank you to the Institute of Policy Studies for giving me this platform to speak on new forms and movements, to talk about what's happening in the environment space, specifically in the climate scene. Like many of you, I have learnt a lot from my fellow speakers about what they have been doing in their various organisations, in different hats and roles, in how they are trying to facilitate conversations, to influence society, and also to effect changes that are necessary to bring us to a better Singapore tomorrow.

I would like to put on my hat as an active volunteer in the environmental space here in Singapore and share with you some of my learnings and observations that I have made through the years. So I'm not just going to talk about my organisation, Singapore Youth for Climate Action, I'm also going to give you a very big-picture view of what's going on in the climate scene here and share with you some examples of what the other groups are doing as well. I have divided my presentation into three parts.

THREE OBSERVATIONS ON THE EVOLUTION OF CLIMATE MOVEMENT IN SINGAPORE

We can examine the climate movement in Singapore in three phases. First, 2010 and 2015; then 2016 to 2018; and last, 2019 to 2020. It is important to first acknowledge that the environment space in Singapore has already been active way before the year 2000, with organisations like Nature Society Singapore and Singapore Environmental Council doing significant work for nature protection and nature conservation here in Singapore. In my opinion, the climate scene really sparked off in 2010.

To give you a bit of context of what was happening globally, this organisation called 350.org, headquartered in the United States, had mobilised thousands of people globally in more than 180 countries, asking people to join its climate movement — to challenge the systems that created the climate crisis. That happened in 2007, and by 2010, it reached Singapore. So the local chapter, 350 in Singapore, started to organise some events. You know people have different ways of advocating for climate policies for climate change. To give a bit of comparison and flavour, in other countries, people were using arts and performance, for instance, or they were talking about organising protests and some were even willing to get arrested for it.

But in Singapore, things were a bit safer. 350 Singapore focused on drilling that sustainability mind-set, in organising outreach talks, documentaries screenings, tree planting, beach clean-ups, youth workshops — really to raise climate awareness first, which I think in that period was not really there yet. Which then brings me to the next period, 2016 to 2018.

Just before that, in 2015, my friends and I who were already volunteering with different organisations in Singapore in the environmental space — we realised that hey, you know, we have already learnt so much about what's happening in the green sector, blue sector, brown sector, and what we are really interested to know about is how countries are addressing these climate issues. So we focused on the United Nations Framework Convention on Climate Change (UNFCCC). We saw that there was an opportunity for us to form a group called Singapore Youth for Climate Action, and this group will organise capacity-building workshops to equip people for that kind of conference. So that started to happen in 2015.

At the same time, I would also like to acknowledge that local academics at the National University of Singapore (which received observer status to the UNFCCC) were also sending staff and students to the UN conferences. With all these different groups going to the UNFCCC — in 2016 and 2018 — we saw that there was a growing interest in people who were not only interested in just knowing about climate change, but really wanted to understand the policies, international negotiations and agreements, and how we could address this at a more systemic level.

This brings me to the third phase of what was happening in the climate scene here in Singapore. To me, the defining moment for us was really last year, when a new group called SG Climate Rally came up and they organised the first-ever climate gathering at Hong Lim Park. This gathering at Hong Lim Park was the first of its kind in Singapore, with people gathering physically to show their concerns for the climate. *The Straits Times* reported about 2,000 in attendance, so really the whole field was filled with people — and mostly young people.

And then this year, I think just last week, it was announced that this group, SG Climate Rally, together with another group, Speak for Climate got together and teamed up for a campaign called Greenwatch. Greenwatch is a climate scorecard to assess all political parties' manifestos and to rank how different parties are addressing the climate crisis. And the aim really is to deepen that climate commitment during the upcoming general election. I also understand that SG Climate Rally has talked to parties like the Singapore Democratic Party and Singapore People's Party for potential collaborations, and if anyone's interested, please contact them.

So I hope you can see from the three time periods that I have shared, that we have moved on from just organising outreach events to now trying to understand policies and negotiations. We want to see how we can change things at a more systemic level and at a faster rate. How can we do that? In this day and age it really is through social media.

TWO EXAMPLES OF HOW SOCIAL MEDIA IS AMPLIFYING THE CLIMATE MOVEMENT IN SINGAPORE

I like to use Facebook, I find it a meaningful platform to engage people to understand what they think about climate change. What are some of their perceptions of policies that are out there? It can really be an interesting space and you really need to control yourself and not be easily triggered. So for me I really like to check out the comments on Green & Clean Singapore's Facebook page. And I sometimes visit news sites like *Today*, CNA, *The Straits Times*, because I think the crowd that comments online are usually not same crowd that I get to meet offline — and I think that's a very important learning space for me. Some people use Telegram and Whatsapp chats to maybe discuss or push alerts notifications, so if you are interested, you can find group chats for food waste and dumpster diving, for instance. These can also be really engaging groups for you to then slowly get into the environment or climate scene.

I would like to shift your attention to a few examples that have been gaining traction in Singapore. In Singapore, we have many active Instagram users and in 2018 we began to see ministries like the Ministry of Finance engaging social media influencers to promote Budget 2018.

I would like to highlight these two users whom I think use Instagram, especially the Instagram story's function, very meaningfully. So first is Tingkats.SG run by Pamela Low, and the second one is theweirdandwild run by Qiyun. For Tingkats.SG, Pamela's style is really understated — show, don't tell. When she attends an event or reads an article and shares with you some of the sustainability angles she learns, she then invites you to converse with her and she shares your comments or stories on her stories. So that's Pamela's style.

For theweirdandwild, Qiyun does very good and quirky illustrations, letting you know the big stuff like sustainable living, climate policies at the local and international levels, where she breaks them down into very quirky illustrations that are simple and easy to understand. I think that's something that we really need, for people to understand it at a simple level and make them want to take action easily.

The next example that I wanted to share on is podcast. I think podcasts as a whole are a growing trend, in the United States and the United Kingdom, even in Singapore, to give you a scale of how big this can be. In the local climate context, we have Audrey Tan and David Fogarty from *The Straits Times*. They launched an environmental series podcast called Green Pulse. We also have CNA 938 "Heart of the Matter", covering some environmental news including the latest UNFCCC.

So a lot of things are going on and I feel social media is the way to go in terms of amplifying the climate education here in Singapore. This brings me to my third section on ignorance, criticism and working together.

Today, with the growing climate movement offline and online, in my ideal state of mind I would like to think that everyone in Singapore is now aware and they want to do something for the climate. And this has been illustrated in surveys published recently — surveys done by National Climate Change Secretariat, by National Youth Council, by Mediacorp even; and generally they say the same thing. Nine out of 10 people in Singapore are aware of climate change, which sounds good, but at the end of the day for me, there're really two issues. The first is that being aware does not necessarily mean you would want to do something to change your behaviour for the climate; and second, it's a very small subset, sample population.

At the end of the day there are still people who are not aware of these things, or maybe they don't read as much, and maybe they don't want to do anything about it. So I think all the more, in the efforts that I share with you, — those by ground up groups and those that are happening on social media — it's important to reduce that gap between having that sympathy for climate issue and being empathetic about it.

IGNORANCE, CRITICISM AND WORKING TOGETHER

There's also the problem of trying to do what we think is best for our country and still being criticised for various things. Associate Professor Winston Chow, currently with the Singapore Management University, has contributed a lot to the climate scene here in Singapore. He was selected by the United Nations' Intergovernmental Panel on Climate Change (IPCC) to contribute to the UN International Climate Report, so he's a very credible person. He gave an interview to Mothership.SG and was criticised for various reasons on social media.

No matter how credible we think we are or how sound we think our policies are, at the end of the day, there will still be critique — and critique that we need to dissect and to understand that they come from a place of concern, and maybe we just need to listen to one another better. How can we do that?

There is one sort of learning that I really want to share here. Last year, I attended a lecture by Yale University's Benjamin Cashore here in Singapore and he is the guy to go to if you really want to learn about policy, and how to address "wicked problems" in policies. He lists and categorises these "wicked problems". Climate change is categorised as a type 4, "super wicked problems". So the idea is, when you want to solve certain issues, you have to identify them correctly, use certain approaches or certain policies, and then from there you can handle things better. Cashore raises three interesting questions: i) how can we design policies that create immediate stickiness such that it cannot be reversed easily; ii) how can we design policies that can be

> So here, regardless of your political leanings and role in society, be it in government or NGOs, I hope you see that the larger cause here is really to work towards a better Singapore. So put aside your differences, and work with each other more.

entrenched and gain support over-time; and iii) how can we design policies that expand the population that supports those policies.

I think these are the kinds of questions we read to ourselves when we are addressing certain things and when we are trying to convince our critics. There can be many different conversations as to what good politics is, and there can be many different angles in terms of freedom of expression or barriers to entry. For me, in the climate context here in Singapore, good politics means having a healthy ecosystem where all the key stakeholders, all the ground up groups, agencies like National Youth Council, and so on, can come together — and we can talk out things with one another, building trust and partnership, which was mentioned earlier this morning.

One thing is clear, regardless of your political affiliation, the climate crisis should be at the top of your agenda and the incumbent should call for national unity when co-creating policies for the climate crisis. Mr Chiam See Tong, he mentioned this in 1984 after his electoral victory[1], and I think it is also appropriate in our current context. He said, whenever possible, he would cooperate with the PAP and find solutions to problems. Mr Chiam said, "I want to help PAP in its responsibility of nation-building.". So here, regardless of your political leanings and role in society, be it in government or NGOs, I hope you see that the larger cause here is really to work towards a better Singapore. So put aside your differences, and work with each other more.

POST-SCRIPT

At the time of writing, it has been seven months since my speech at Singapore Perspectives held on 20 January 2020. Numerous events have taken place in between, and in this piece, I would like to bring to your attention to two significant events: COVID-19 and the Singapore General Election. In this reflection, I would like to make linkages between those two

---

[1] For details, see www.todayonline.com/big-read/big-read-short-examining-mr-chiam-see-tongs-legacy

events and with two of the points I made in my speech: in the introduction, on the evolution of the climate movement in Singapore; and in the conclusion, on putting aside differences to work together towards a larger cause.

COVID-19 and the evolution of the climate movement in Singapore

Many articles have been published to reflect the relationship and the consequences between COVID-19 and climate change.[2] Several people made similar observations that the disruption to food supplies as well as employment brought about by the pandemic are scenarios that can be brought about by a climate emergency too.[3] Others commented that we should take this global crisis as an opportunity to green the financial system and build a more climate-resilient Singapore. It has also been reported that COVID-19 has hindered some green infrastructure projects here.[4]

At this point of reflecting on all these commentaries, what I find beautiful in this predicament we are in is how people in Singapore are responding to COVID-19. Besides the support schemes introduced by various agencies, support groups initiated by ordinary people have sprouted in the past months as well. For the former, I suggest visiting Support Go Where[5] and for the latter COVID-19 Mutual Aid Hub Singapore[6] to find out more.

I know there are times where I have been cynical about things, but I will also be the first to say that I believe Singapore does have a first-class government, and a first-class public service. In the same vein, I also believe we have one of the most educated, compassionate, and efficient societies. Therefore, when faced with the full-blown impacts of climate change in the near future, I have trust that our people will self-organise and support one another just like how we are doing with COVID-19. Yes, we can come up with all the technical solutions in the world and attempt to minimise climate

---

[2] For example, see https://www.channelnewsasia.com/news/commentary/covid-19-coronavirus-climate-change-clear-skies-pollution-animal-12757348
[3] For example, see www.straitstimes.com/singapore/environment/covid-19-crisis-not-a-solution-to-climate-change-but-a-learning-opportunity
[4] For details, see https://www.channelnewsasia.com/news/singapore/climate-change-goals-singapore-covid-19-13025696
[5] For details, see www.supportgowhere.gov.sg
[6] For details, see https://aidhubsg.com/

impacts but it is the social awareness and social interactions that will keep us together. Maybe we have yet to feel how strong the climate movement can be in Singapore. It is growing and I believe it will be even stronger.

If this were a social media post, this is the part where I use #SGUnited #SingaporeTogether.

Singapore General Election and putting aside differences to work together towards a larger cause

A funny thing happened on the afternoon of 22 June 2020. I emailed my Member of Parliament to ask some constituency-related matters. That same evening, I emailed some ministers a four-page PDF listing questions I had for the Emerging Stronger Taskforce, Regional Comprehensive Economic Partnership (RCEP), and Singapore's Contribution to Carbon Emissions Overseas. I did not know it was going to happen of course but the very next day Prime Minister Lee Hsien Loong called for the General Election (GE) to take place on 10 July. At that point it meant the Parliament was dissolved and I knew I was not going to receive replies till much later.

In retrospect, those two weeks leading up to GE was possibly the most emotional period for me as a Singaporean in 2020. I remember being on Instagram stories a lot and sharing snippets of my thoughts. I was pointing out how unfair certain parts of various systems were. I was reading up on the various political parties and tried to understand where they were coming from and what they wanted. I even ended up volunteering as a Counting Agent for a political party that was contesting in my constituency. The political party was clear they were engaging us as regular citizens and that we were not party members. I was clear that I wanted to do it on the basis I wanted to support an organisation with far less resources, and I wanted to play my part as a citizen to ensure the votes were counted properly. I have mentioned this to a few people as well that I liked parts of their Green Charter, and again in retrospect, I felt that contributed to me feeling I volunteered my time meaningfully.

Fast-forward to 25 July and PM Lee announced a new Cabinet. More notably for the context of this piece, Mr Masagos Zulkifli who was Minister for the Environment and Water Resources was appointed Minister for Social and Family Development and Second Minister for Health. He remains the Minister-in-charge of Muslim Affairs. Meanwhile Ms Grace Fu was appointed Minister for Sustainability and the Environment.[7] She relinquished her appointment as Minister for Culture, Community and Youth. That change in political leadership hit me.

On one level, it hit me how even within the same political party an individual will not always be the one in charge of a specific portfolio. Essentially, these are assigned jobs. Objectively, whoever is assigned to it will have to just pick up what is on the plate and deliver even more.

On another level, it hit me how now there is always a call for citizens to engage with the ministries and agencies, to be part of some focus group discussions, or to have some sort of partnerships. There are days where I just lament to my close friends how at times I feel it had been superficial of me in the past decade to focus on community outreach and event organising to promote climate awareness. And now this was happening. Yes the climate advocacy was happening, people are engaged, but I mean really, how does this all contribute to reducing carbon emissions at source?

That said, I think that is the point. Regardless of the changing situations or leaderships, regardless of our roles in society, we need to take up some responsibility to address climate change, and we need to push for more change. Individually we may not feel we are creating impact, but with more people, we definitely can. There may be some highs and lows, some great moments and some frictions. But hey, tensions within oneself and differences with others can be a force for good, so let us use that as an advantage to build a more sustainable Singapore.

---

[7] The Ministry of the Environment and Water Resources was renamed the Ministry of Sustainability and the Environment.

CHAPTER 9

Three Hypotheses on Keeping Singapore Going, Growing and Glowing

CHAN CHUN SING

In many places, "politics" is almost a dirty word, often associated with a power contest for one's personal benefit and almost always associated with corruption. Hence, not surprisingly, in many of these places, many of the most capable and committed have hesitated to come forth to serve in political service.

In Singapore, politics is about governance. Governance is fundamentally about improving the lives of our people, and allowing them the best opportunities to fulfil their potential and aspirations. To enable this, we have to carry out the difficult task of building a political system and culture that will keep Singapore going, growing and glowing. Many other societies are fracturing under the stresses and strains of various forces. Some are unable to help their enterprises and workers make the necessary adjustments brought about by globalisation and technological disruptions. Others are appealing to the narrow interests of specific groups, fracturing the political centre and making difficult the need for balance and compromise. There is also political opportunism of both the extreme left and the extreme right to exploit the fears of people in a volatile and uncertain environment. In Singapore, we face a major challenge as an open society as external forces will always try to influence our choices and directions. Unlike many other countries, we do not have the geographical, historical, linguistic or cultural buffers against many of these external forces.

I would like to propose three hypotheses on how Singapore can remain exceptional amidst global and local developments.

SINGAPORE'S POLITICAL DNA

My first hypothesis: To remain exceptional and keep going, we must have a political DNA that inclines us to constructive solutioning and positive actions beyond rhetoric and debate.

Some define democracy too narrowly as contention among opposing and competing ideologies. Indeed, in many parts of the world, this is a popular definition. Others suggest that the mark of success is about the quantity of different voices and representations in the legislature for society. These definitions are inadequate.

Beyond plurality, any functioning political system must have reasoned debate based on facts that lead to concrete actions and plans to better the lives of the people. What distinguishes Singapore is the second part of the sentence — that beyond reasoned debate based on facts, we need concrete plans and actions to improve the lives of our people. This is the essence of SG Together.

In this digital age of fake news and alternative reality, this simple task has never been harder. Beyond plurality, there must be mechanisms to allow the diversity of ideas and the divergence of perspectives to finally lead to convergence for action. This is the true test of democracy in action.

In many societies and democracies, we indeed see plurality and diversity today. But we have yet to see many societies where all of these lead to convergence in action. Instead, increasingly we see compromises and consideration for the broader societal interests giving way to narrow sectoral interests. The result being that the longer-term interests of future generations are often sacrificed. It is as if politics is only for me, here and now. The future voter is absent and mostly ignored.

We, especially the young, will really have to ask ourselves this: what sort of politics do we want, if Singapore is to be around forever, not just for the next four to five years?

STAYING RELEVANT WITH NEEDS

The second hypothesis: To keep Singapore growing, we will need to have the gumption to evolve our political system to stay relevant with the needs of the time.

It is an arduous task, but the lack of evolution in any system almost inevitably leads to revolution. The system ossifies and collapses. Certainly, no political system is perfect for all times. Functioning political systems are always works-in-progress.

In Singapore's context, be it the GRC system, elected presidency, or POFMA (Protection from Online Falsehoods and Manipulation Act), all of us have a responsibility to ask how we should evolve our systems-to anticipate and pre-empt problems even when it is politically inconvenient and politically not expedient. We have seen examples in other countries where political systems become outdated, unable to represent the aspirations of their people and unable to deliver the results for the current generation. Can Singapore avoid this fate? Can maturity in our case not be a prelude to ossification, decrepitude, and finally collapse? I will posit that the answers to these questions are as important as who we choose to lead us within the existing system.

POLITICAL ETHOS

My third and final hypothesis: To keep Singapore glowing beyond culture and structure, the final piece must be the ethos of political leadership.

How do we inspire and bring forth teams of people who are capable, committed, and full of conviction? People who will uphold values and be prepared to make bold, difficult, but necessary decisions. People with the vision and ability to anticipate challenges and more importantly to take them on ahead of time. People with the gumption to lead and not just see where everyone is running, sprint ahead of them, and for good measure shout "follow me". That means we need good and real political leaders and not just politicians for the short haul.

We have been lucky over the last six decades, but maintaining the right ethos of political service will never be easy, especially in times of peace and

All of us are leaders in our respective circles of influence. All of us will have the responsibility to be part of the solution, part of the effort to seek those solutions.

> True political service requires leadership and stewardship for this generation and for the future generations. The emphasis is on "service" and not "politics".

abundance. We can all be easily lulled into complacency thinking that "all will be well" or that someone else can do the job. This issue however goes beyond political leadership. It actually applies to leadership at all levels of society!

All of us are leaders in our respective circles of influence. All of us will have the responsibility to be part of the solution, part of the effort to seek those solutions.

As fellow Singaporeans, we have the same shared responsibility to seek solutions for the challenges that we face, anticipate the challenges that we face and put in place systems, structures, organisations, cultures ahead of time and pre-empt those challenges.

True political service requires leadership and stewardship for this generation and for the future generations. The emphasis is on "service" and not "politics". May we all work together as one united team to keep Singapore going, growing and glowing!

Key Moments of Q&A

This chapter contains a selection of exchanges during the question-and-answer segments of the conference.[1] They have been organised according to themes, based on our reading of the questions that were asked and the responses given. We hope that organising these exchanges in this manner will provide readers with the rich perspectives that came from different speakers on the same themes. There were many questions and insightful exchanges, but due to space constraints, we were unable to include every one of them. Instead, we have prioritised exchanges that are aligned to the topic of politics as well as their connections to other questions and responses.

Deputy Prime Minister Heng Swee Keat and Minister Chan Chun Sing had their own dialogue sessions, so the questions were posed directly to them. For all other speakers, questions were often presented in a manner that was directed at the speakers in each panel, i.e., Lam Peng Er, Zuraidah Ibrahim and Bilahari Kausikan in Section I; Crystal Abidin, Cai Yinzhou, Carrie Tan and Nor Lastrina Hamid in Section II. Where possible, questions have been identified with the individuals who asked them, although this is not always the case as some participants did not identify themselves.

---

[1] Please visit our website for the full videos of the question-and-answer segments and SP2020 itself: https://lkyspp.nus.edu.sg/news-events/events/details/singapore-perspectives-2020-politics

On challenges facing Singapore:

Question (Q): DPM, you spoke about the challenges that we will face in the foreseeable future. What do you think is our biggest political challenge?

Heng Swee Keat:

You will see rising geopolitical uncertainties. I mentioned that in the earlier period after the Second World War, there was support for multilateralism and free trade. The advanced economies were growing very well and they, in turn, cascaded their technology and skills, and many developing countries caught up.

The world progressed together, in a very synergistic way, and everyone benefited from this. Indeed, corporations and investors ventured out, and developing countries have all benefited hugely from this. Singapore is a very good example.

But, over time, the developing countries are catching up, their companies are growing, and the gap is no longer so clear. In many places, structural changes in the global economy and in their economies have not taken place. We cannot have a world that continues growing unless all of us make structural changes as other countries adjust. This is something that we must take seriously in Singapore because if other economies restructure, we must think of our new pattern of specialisation and the value-add that we can create to the rest of the world.

But, if that does not take place and workers are not reskilled, the industries will go and the workers who are affected will suffer from that. As a result, you will find that politics all over the world has become a lot more difficult.

You will find that instead of a world of cooperation and globalisation, you will now see a world in greater conflict. The geopolitical strategic challenges are going to be significant, underpinned by the changing economic weights and also, this is spilling over to the competition in technology because in the age of the Fourth Industrial Revolution, everyone recognises that the future of countries and the future of

> By staying united, Singaporeans have shown time and again that we can beat the odds and continue to be exceptional.
>
> — *Heng Swee Keat*

companies and economies depend on how well you have invested in R&D and how well we are able to make full use of technology.

In the midst of major changes that are going on around us, the question is: Can we stay united and draw strength from our diversity, draw strength from each other, so that we can continue to progress together? By staying united, Singaporeans have shown time and again that we can beat the odds and continue to be exceptional.

Q: Good evening Minister Chan, I am Chin How from Temasek Junior College. I just want to ask about your long-term vision for Singapore. Being cognisant of global uncertainty, be it politically, socially or economically, where do you see Singapore in the next 20 to 30 years?

Chan Chun Sing:

My long-term vision in Singapore is not just for the next 20 to 30 years. I grew up in a system, where I understand that the last 50 over years of our existence has been an aberration in the history of Singapore and the history of this part of the world. If we go back a few hundred years, Singapore has never been independent and some would argue, Singapore has never been allowed to be independent. As a small city-state, without a natural conventional hinterland, it is very difficult to survive. Without those external links for resources, supplies, markets, talent and so forth, it's very difficult.

We have to make a living for ourselves, we have to defend ourselves, take care of our security, we have to earn our keep and not depend on other people's charity. We have to value-add so that we entrench ourselves in the global environment. Nobody has sympathy or charity for a small country. In the last 50 years, we have had to navigate a domestic environment whereby we all came from different shores. That to have a country regardless of race, language, religion, is not the norm. In fact, in many other countries, the national identity has to do with race, language, religion, ancestry, geography and so forth. That's why I say just now, even until today, we don't have the geographical, cultural, linguistic buffers against many of the global forces impacting us.

If we are careless, if we are not careful, if we are not sensitive to the larger forces in the world, if we take what we have for granted, then very easily, we could lose all these and have to start all over again. So I never take it as a given that we will arrive at SG100 effortlessly. Never.

When I went back to the SAF and talked to them, I asked them "How many of you think that we will celebrate SG100 based on the current trajectory?" Many of them put up their hands and I'm very proud of them. But I reminded them, while you have the confidence, and I'm proud that you have the confidence, never forget why you are still in uniform. The very fact that you are still in uniform tells us that we have many other challenges that require you to be in a uniform. And it's not a job done, it's always a work-in-progress.

At MTI, every day my economic team has to go round to the rest of the world and convince people, local and foreign, to put their investments in Singapore so that we can have good and better jobs for our people — not just for today, but for the future. And we have to do that delicate balance. The EDB officers grow up very fast. They grow up learning that nobody will owe us a living, that we have to give a value proposition to the rest of the world on why they need to do business with us.

When it comes to social issues, we have succeeded on many fronts. But the challenges are ongoing. In the past, we were equally poor. Today, we are unequally rich. The challenges are no less. In the past, everybody feels that they have a chance to rise up to the top. And today, we pride ourselves still, that amongst all the societies that we see, Singapore is probably the best place to be born even if you don't come from a privileged background. Because we have every reason to believe that we can succeed. But that is not to be taken for granted. Every country, as they mature, ossify. Countries form groups and after a while, there will be groups that ask themselves, why should I continue to support this system if I cannot get ahead in this system? Those are our ongoing challenges.

What is my vision? I only have one simple vision for my entire life work, be it in the SAF, MSF, NTUC, or now

> We may not have a common ancestry, race, language and religion, but we can define our identity, based on a forward-looking set of values of multiculturalism, meritocracy, and incorruptibility — that we will define a future where the future is in our hands and we are not beholden to others nor held ransom by others.
>
> — Chan Chun Sing

MTI. That is for Singapore to defy the odds of history, to survive and thrive as a small city-state without a natural hinterland. We may not have a common ancestry, race, language and religion, but we can define our identity, based on a forward-looking set of values of multiculturalism, meritocracy, and incorruptibility — that we will define a future where the future is in our hands and we are not beholden to others nor held ransom by others.

My wife asked me, why do you continue to be where you are? Every day, you are getting all the brickbats. Your family is getting the brickbats. Your children are getting the brickbats. Why are we still here? I am still here because I want my children and my grandchildren and for many more generations to come to be able to call themselves Singaporeans — that they have the means to be called Singaporeans and they have the gumption to be called Singaporeans. The will that today we may just be Singaporeans, but one day there will be a Singapore tribe.

I liked what Indranee proposed as the tagline for our Bicentennial year. "From Singapore to Singaporeans". There's a double meaning to it. From Singapore, a geographical location, to Singaporean, the people. A people united by a set of values although we may not have a common ancestry, race, and religion. But "Singapore to Singaporeans" is also about our stewardship to leave behind something better for the next generation. Just as the previous generations have left us with what we have today — that every generation of Singaporeans will not fear because they will start from a higher platform to scale a higher peak; that every generation will lend our shoulders to the next to stand taller and see further. And if we can continue to do that, I'm not worried about SG100. I will say that even beyond SG100, we will continue to shine.

The next lap for Singapore is not just dependent on a few of us. All of us in this room have the opportunity and the responsibility in our respective circles to build that Singapore that we want. Not just economically, not just from the defence and security perspective, but also culture.

All of you present today are either family, friend, or a fan of Singapore. For those who are Singaporeans, you know this place belongs to us all. And because it belongs to us all, we all have a shared responsibility towards ourselves and future generations. For those who are friends and fans of Singapore, if you believe and you buy into this vision that we have as a small city-state to defy the odds, then may you also join hands with us to bring forth this Singapore that you can be so proud to call yourself friend or fan.

On Singapore Together

Q: Hi DPM, my name is Adriel from Yale-NUS College and I would like to ask about SG Together engagements. How do you ensure that the voices of the lower-income and underrepresented individuals and communities are included in this engagement exercise, such that the SG that we build together for the future is one that is inclusive?

Heng Swee Keat:

This is an excellent question — this is something that we will be very careful in deciding – the various groups who are participating in SG Together.

Just last week, I was in the session with Minister Desmond Lee and a few other Ministers, where we met many of the groups who were working with people with various needs, many social agencies, and we had a very good discussion on some of the things we could do together.

> There will be forums for various groups to make sure that we hear a very diverse set of views, because everyone, as I said, should have a future in Singapore, a stake in Singapore, regardless of your starting point.
>
> — *Heng Swee Keat*

I will say that the outreach must go beyond just the social services agencies. As a Member of Parliament on the ground, I meet many of my residents. Some of them are quite comfortable, some of them need help, and indeed, we will make sure that the sessions that we organise work on that. There will be forums for various groups to make sure that we hear a very diverse set of views, because everyone, as I said, should have a future in Singapore, a stake in Singapore, regardless of your starting point.

Q: I have a question, DPM, about "We" and managing "Differences". Our founding Prime Minister, Mr Lee Kuan Yew, has said that "We" in the Singapore pledge, "We, the citizens of Singapore", which you have mentioned just now, is only an aspiration. While we all continue to work hard on it to make it a reality, what are the challenges? And my question is, are we managing the differences well? For example, I think Mr Janadas mentioned just now that we invited the leader of Opposition, but he declined. Congratulations to the IPS for doing so, but it is a pity that the leader of Opposition declined. But managing differences is not just about Opposition politicians, but people who differ in our views. Are we doing enough in managing those differences in order to remain united, and more than just a question of social cohesion and inequalities?

Heng Swee Keat:
On Ambassador Zainul's question about managing differences and not just about politicians, I will say that you are pointing to a broader set of issues about whether we have enough diversity of views, and are we considering diverse views?

I will say that even in this room — this is an IPS crowd, these are people who come for IPS seminars and are very interested in policy, I am quite certain that even in this group, if you were to do some polls and measures, you will have very different points of views.

The important thing is to make sure that we have the same sets of facts, that we base our arguments on the same sets of truth that we can agree on and look at creative ways to solve the problem. In fact, one of the objectives of Singapore Together is precisely for that.

There are many different ways for us to achieve an objective. Which is better and more sustainable? This is something which we can discuss, and I hope that there will be many more of such discussions about what are the right things, what are the good things that we can do that will be sustainable and how organisations like IPS and universities, are in fact putting out policy options for us to study.

Q: There's a kind of deep, benevolent humanism in what has been said. We are assuming that people want to know, that people want to recognise each other. We are assuming that people want to actually have actual recognition and human contact. Are we right in making that assumption?

Carrie Tan:

On Professor Farish's question about whether it's a good strategy to assume, to take a benevolent approach and assume that everybody wants to, you know, be nice and to love one another, and everybody wants to recognise differences, I think being in the civil society where we are running charities, we are doing social movements, we kind of have the luxury of giving people the benefit of the doubt, and I have to say that with our organisation's experience, that has translated to amazing outcomes as you can see from the success stories we shared.

So I'm hoping that there is room for this kind of stories to inspire some kind of mentality change to shift from a fear-based mentality of policymaking to more love-based or investment, pragmatically speaking, investment-based way of looking at public policy. Often we come across policymakers saying, you know, they don't want to do this or that because they worry about certain schemes or certain provisions being abused. And that's perfectly understandable given that you are under public scrutiny and you are being responsible and accountable to the public.

So I think this kind of question requires us to think about both as citizens and as policymakers. Is this the kind of renegotiation of social contract that we want to have, where we delegate the pragmatism to government and should they make mistakes, you know, the MRT breaks down and we get into a fuss about it right? Or can we also give the confidence and leeway for perhaps policymakers to also adopt some love-based or benevolence-based kind of policymaking?

On divisions

Q: Hello Mr Heng, I am Goh Meng Seng from the People's Power Party. You have talked about divisive forces and about national identity. If you go back to the founding years of Singapore, we actually faced divisive forces also. We also faced divisive forces, because after the war, we have nationalism that comes off from Communist China and Malaysia, right? And we had a big problem to deal with back then. But after 30 years, have we integrated as a core? My question is whether the divisive forces are coming back again. From statistics, when you look at 2007 to 2019, we are giving out about 20,000 new citizenships to people from different countries, especially to Mainland China, Malaysia, India, and Philippines. Where will they stand when we have to make a difficult decision in geopolitics? Will this affect our policies, our political directions, and the decisions that we make, and will they exert their thoughts to be pro-China, pro-Philippines, or pro-India?

Heng Swee Keat:
Let me address Mr Goh Meng Seng's question about whether having new citizens will end up as a sort of new divisive force. It can be, if we exploit it and start casting doubts on the loyalties and the fitness of new citizens and all that. We will create a new divide.

As I mentioned in my speech earlier on, one in three marriages today involves a Singaporean and a citizen of another country, and we have to bear that in mind. In fact, as a Member of Parliament, at every of my Meet-the-People Session, I have some Singaporeans, men and women, who will come to me and say, "I married so and so from this country, and can I get the citizenship for my wife or my husband quickly?"

We must bear in mind, for those people who have become Singapore citizens, they have become citizens by conviction. They have left their country and decided that Singapore is a better place for them and their children in the future.

We should, as Singaporeans, make the best effort to integrate them — to integrate them into our society, to welcome them, so that they can be part of our team. In that regard, I must say that I am very troubled that so many people are seeking to exploit these differences. Instead of making the effort to integrate them, they have made this into an issue and they have made this into a "you are not taking care of Singaporeans, you are not taking care of Singaporeans' interests" scenario.

On the contrary, having new citizens is very much part of our effort to take care of Singaporeans. There are many business leaders in this room here and I can tell you the number of sessions that I go to when doing the work on the Future Economy, on how many times they have been telling me how hard it is to grow their companies in Singapore. Because our criteria for bringing in foreigners on an employment, work, or special pass, is tighter with the foreign worker levy.

> But, if we take a narrow nativist approach, and say that let us keep out the world, let us keep out trade, let us keep out other people, then eventually, Singapore will wither.
> — *Heng Swee Keat*

These measures are to ensure that we also take care of the interests of Singaporeans. Having the foreigners in our midst adds to our strength.

There is another aspect, which is worthwhile for all of us to bear in mind, especially the younger ones in this room. I mentioned the age of global uncertainty and the age of disruption. One important way that Singaporeans can excel and thrive in this world, in this age of uncertainty, is to make sure that we grow up in a multi-racial, multi-religious, multi-lingual society, and that ought to give us a very high degree of cultural sensitivity.

I met a group of young students the other day and a few of them had foreign students as their friends in their class. They told me about the learning that they had — about other countries and cultures, particularly those in South East Asia, and it has been a very enriching experience. I felt very cheered by that because when they grow up, they will be in a good position to interact with our friends in ASEAN, Asia, and all over the world, and that gives Singaporeans an edge.

Even when you travel, you have to carry different adapter plugs because some have two-pins or three-pins, and some are square or circle. Singaporeans should be like adapter plugs to be carried all over, wherever we go, we can plug in and draw energy and link up with all.

Having that cultural sensitivity and respect for people from all over the world will give us a very special edge, especially in a world where people are turning inwards, in a world where people are less willing to cooperate, Singaporeans can extend a hand, we can be bridge-builders in a more fragmented world.

The key point is that, whatever we do, must be to take care of Singaporeans and Singapore's future. But, if we take a narrow nativist approach, and say that let us keep out the world, let us keep out trade, let us keep out other people, then eventually, Singapore will wither.

Q: Where do you see yourself, your own work and what you are doing, and how does your work, you know, contribute to this understanding that society — and in this case Singaporeans' society — is not this flat, homogeneous space, but it's actually something extremely complex? And is there worth in doing this, do you think it's important to emphasise this complexity?

Cai Yinzhou:

So with regard to complexity, I think in the migrant workers' space, it is a complex topic to discuss, because many of them will be perceived as non-Singaporeans and therefore may not be acceded the right platforms for this cause. But one of the things that I have learned is also in terms of our interdependence with this group of people, for example in terms of our, much of our care nursing homes or many of the jobs that they fill are completely dependent on the pool of foreign workers within our midst. So this interdependence is also recognised not just in the jobs that

> So that's also something that hopefully can be a social norm that changes over time as we have more opportunities to integrate, with social media being one of the levellers for these changes and these platforms where people can actually voice out about their lives and their human stories. And I think that that brings across a solidarity point where everyone can come together and acknowledge their struggles regardless of the jobs or backgrounds they have in society.
> — *Cai Yinzhou*

they fill but also historically how we have come to be — as a nation that has embraced the diversity and strengths of different individuals from different backgrounds. And it is also a very pragmatic way of integrating people for the purpose of the better good of all of who come to Singapore to find work.

So I think in terms of politics, it is quite divisive. When you talk about nationality, many of us do see them as "others". Unfortunately, it's also something that is perpetuated by some of our parent's generation, for example, they tell me, you know, don't hang out with them, and the stereotypes that these populations have. So that's also something that hopefully can be a social norm that changes over time as we have more opportunities to integrate, with social media being one of the levellers for these changes and these platforms where people can actually voice out about their lives and their human stories. And I think that that brings across a solidarity point where everyone can come together and acknowledge their struggles regardless of the jobs or backgrounds they have in society.

On Singapore's democracy and political system

Q: Hello DPM, I am Leong Mun Wai from the Progress Singapore Party. However, the questions I am going to ask and the opinions expressed are my own. I have three short questions.

First, diversity has been a common topic today, we have talked a lot about diversity, and diversity is something that is a norm as our society develops. Given that Parliament already has the NCMP and the NMP schemes, is there a plan or consideration to move into a proportional representation in our Parliament?

Second, given the recent changes to the elected presidency, there is a feeling that the effectiveness of the system as a check and balance on the Executive is curtailed because most importantly, the eligibility criteria has been toughened, as a result, there will only be a handful of Singaporeans who are eligible to stand for the presidential election.

Third, many Singaporeans would like to know, given the state of development of our country, we have become a first world country in terms of economic attainment, how does our government position our nation in the world in the next 10, 30, and 50 years? There is some thinking that Singapore is still only a mercantile nation. Thank you.

Heng Swee Keat:

Now we have looked at systems around the world, and in every system, you will find that there are issues, there is no perfect system. And whether you end up with proportional representation or not, does it lead to a better airing of views? It may or may not.

But what is important, as Ambassador Zainul mentioned earlier, is how we ensure that different viewpoints can be brought to the discussions in our public discourse. This discussion and the many different forums that IPS has been organising are very helpful for us to discuss social, economic, or political issues.

If we open our minds, we will find that there are plenty of opinions that are being aired in Singapore and around the world. You have access to the internet and to global newspapers, and you see that proliferation of views is not missing. But what is important is that we do not end up with polarisation and extreme views that are being purveyed by the different groups.

The second question about changes in the EP — that checks and balances have been curtailed, I really do not understand the basis for you saying that. In fact, the president has a very important custodial role and before I can even introduce the Supply Bill in government, I have to assure the elected president that this Budget is not likely to draw on past reserves. And every year, when the Auditor-General has completed the work, I have to certify to the elected president that this year, the Auditor-General has confirmed that I, as Finance Minister, has not drawn on past reserves. So, the protection framework that we have, the custodial role that the president is playing, is functioning well.

Now, your final question on whether we are a mercantile nation. Again, I do not understand what you mean by mercantile nation, but if you are asking if we trade with other people, we do. Do we just take a narrow view and say that, I will trade with you only if it benefits me? Well, trade is the free exchange of goods and services and we trade because both parties benefit from it. Singapore's trade is three times our GDP, I do not think we can afford to be selective.

Q: What do you think are current needs? What do you have in mind or what is your vision of an evolved political system which is not only what 4G leaders are thinking but will be welcomed by 4G or 5G population? The second one is on political leadership. We have always been told about the importance of strong political leadership in Singapore. Yet on the other hand, we are also told that it's getting much more difficult now for PAP to attract good people into politics. How do you think this will impact on the quality of our leadership, political leadership, and quality of the Cabinet?

Chan Chun Sing:
There are three dimensions that I personally would like to see in the evolution of our own political system and culture.

Firstly, our own internal discussion and debate. Increasingly, we have a more educated population. Their capacity to absorb and understand the issues facing us has correspondingly increased. It has always been my own personal desire that we have more in-depth discussions with our own people on the challenges facing us. While our education system is very well structured and has achieved much, I always feel that we lack in-depth discussions with our own people on the challenges facing us. This was the reason why since I came into politics — I started a monthly closed-door session that only Singaporeans attend, to share challenges facing us, the choices that we have, and the trade-offs that we have to consider. My aim is not to tell Singaporeans what the solutions are. The challenges will evolve. It is more important for fellow Singaporeans to understand the considerations behind the answer than the answer itself. My hope is that as time goes by, as the circumstances change, we will also evolve our solutioning. There is no one problem where we can ever say that this is the answer and this answer will be eternally correct or relevant. The question is how do we scale up this level of in-depth discussions with fellow Singaporeans? Many of the issues confronting us from security to economics and social may not be so easily discussed in open sessions with other people beyond Singaporeans. Many people have told me that they enjoyed the sessions they have with me. They come to understand why we choose certain courses of action and not others because they have gone through the thinking process.

The second dimension has got to do with the external forces that we have to contend with. The more successful we are in Singapore, sometimes we become very inward looking. We start to talk about all the trade-offs and balances that have to be done domestically. I would be really worried if we were to lose that consciousness of what is happening to the external world. For example, EDB and MTI announced we have secured more than S$15 billion worth of investments last year, so that in the next few years, there will be a stream of investments coming into the economy, creating good and better jobs for Singaporeans. Very soon, we hear feedback and conversations asking why we chose all these investments and why must we take them all. Now these are valid questions but what belies this set of questions perhaps, is a lack of appreciation of the external environment that we are operating in. It is not as if that we have a choice to pick one investment and not another investment. In fact, we didn't get all the investments that we want. We have lost some to our competitors. Our competitors are also not static. They are also doing as much as they can to win those investments over. So that's on the economic side.

As for the geopolitical, defence and security aspects, there are often very sensitive issues that are more difficult for us to discuss publicly. But how do we have many of these sessions to allow our people to have a sense of the dynamics behind the scene? I don't know whether you all are familiar with this IT platform called vTaiwan. It is an internet platform that they are trying to use at scale, whereby they try to gather the views of the entire society, not just to debate but to bring them to convergence for actions. I watch this with a lot of interest because I've always wondered how can we scale up our discussions with our fellow Singaporeans on many of these difficult decisions we have to make.

The third dimension has got to do with the future. Whenever we make decisions for the country in this generation, it doesn't just affect the people in this generation. We need to have a perspective of how it affects the future generation. But in almost every society that we come across, the future voter is absent. An example would be the management of our reserves. These are issues that cut across different generations and we need to find a mechanism whereby our generation makes decisions not just for the sole purview of taking care of this generation.

We have the good fortune because our forefathers have the kind of values to leave us with what we have today. Changi Airport, for example, was literally built by the previous generation with their resources and left to us. Whereas in many other countries you go to an airport or big infrastructure projects, it will inevitably be by borrowing from or taxation from the current generation. Very few societies have this privilege whereby the generation not only takes care of their own generation but leaves behind something for the next generation too.

The question is, as our society becomes older and the physical pressures become tougher, will we be able to continue to maintain this ethos and culture in our society? Will we always in every generation say that when we make a decision it is not just for this generation but also with a view of the next generation?

Now on your second question, you mentioned about the difficulty to attract good people. First let me

In fact, the challenges faced by the previous generations were no less challenging. Every generation will have to navigate and find good people to come forth and serve. When I say good, I don't just mean intellectually good, but most importantly with the right values and with the right teamwork. Running a country can never be done by any single man or woman, no matter how good he or she may be.

— *Chan Chun Sing*

caveat this. I don't want it to sound as though only this generation has problems trying to attract people into political service. In fact, the challenges faced by the previous generations were no less challenging. Every generation will have to navigate and find good people to come forth and serve. When I say good, I don't just mean intellectually good, but most importantly with the right values and with the right teamwork. Running a country can never be done by any single man or woman, no matter how good he or she may be.

So the first order of business is, how do you get people with the right values in? To the best of our efforts we may still get it wrong, and sometimes people come in and they change, now these are all the risks of selecting people to come forth and encouraging them to come forth to serve.

Once they are in, how do we gel them into a coherent team? That they do not love themselves more than they love the country. Those are the critical challenges. As to how does it make a difference to how the Cabinet relates to the public? No, I don't think so. How the Cabinet, executives, the Legislature relate to the public, I don't think it will change that fundamentally. Every Member of Parliament, regardless of which party you are from, you are expected to keep a very close pace, close touch with the ground.

We don't run a system like some other countries whereby some of the executive members are not Members of Parliament. That means they don't have responsibilities on the ground. Those countries with those systems, they have some pluses but they also have a lot of minuses. Some pluses are that their Ministers will be able to focus on what they call the national duties and then they leave the MPs to manage the ground. But you have a divide between what the Ministers in the Cabinet think versus what the ground feels.

In Singapore, our system requires those two duties to be fused into one. It also has its pluses and minuses. The plus is that unlike the rest, we have a better feel of the ground issues and concerns because every one of us has to run our own constituencies. Well you can argue that the minus is that it makes it very challenging for the same person to do the two at the same time. For example, if you happen to be the foreign minister, you are expected to run around, travel around the world and make sure that you secure and defend our interests there. How do you do that and balance that with the need to take care of your own constituency? I don't think just because you are the Minister of Foreign Affairs, people will give you a discount in their expectations locally.

There are pluses and minuses in either system. But the strength of our system must be that our leaders must always keep their feet firmly planted on the ground, keep their ears close to the ground to understand what are the fears, concerns and aspirations of our people. At the same time, when it comes to difficult decisions, they must build trust with our people, share with them the challenges and then take the difficult decisions collectively.

Q: My question is kind of a historical and contemporary one. The Indonesian Chief Security Minister, has said that they are going to revive the Truth and Reconciliation Commission regarding the 1965 massacres that took place in Indonesia. So my question is whether there is any chance at all that there will be a similar commission looking at the Operation Coldstore in 1963. And before you ask me what's the point of the question, the point of the question is that Dr Lim Hock Siew was a very good family friend of my parents, and I think that his family deserves to have a hearing.

Chan Chun Sing:
So Paul[2], the first question is will we have that? I don't know. The rest of the society will have to decide. But let me say this, I worked in Indonesia for two years. I wouldn't comment on who's right and who's wrong. But in 1965, or what happened in the 1960s for that matter, there are deep, deep implications on the psyche of the Indonesians. And there's a history beyond that even. But I don't think it will be appropriate for us to compare that with what you say Operation Coldstore. I think the Indonesians will be quite offended to hear us comparing that because the implications on the society between this and that, I'm not sure is the same. And I generally try not to do this kind of cross-country comparison. Now today I hear you, you believe that the family of Mr Lim Hock Siew has a story to share and I don't think today Mr Lim is unable to share his stories. And then Singaporeans in future, now and in future will have to judge whether the actions taken were appropriate or not appropriate. So I will leave it at that.

---

[2] Dr Paul Tambyah from the Singapore Democratic Party.

Q: My question is more related to non-partisanship. Will we ever see a Singapore where we do not have parties in Parliament? So it's about an evolving structure. And if yes, why? And if no, why?

Chan Chun Sing:

I agree with you, to be exceptional, we cannot just be so on the economics, political fronts. What can Singapore do in a world that may be fragmenting and bifurcating culturally? If we want to create niche value-added prepositions to the rest of the world, then we must have this capability to help integrate different parts together. We can't do that unless we have the cultural quotient as you seemed to suggest — for us to understand and bring people together. Singapore does have quite a good reputation on the international circuit to bring people together. Because we are small and not threatening, and we genuinely believe in a world whereby it's better for everybody to come and work together. We will need to play our part. We will need to develop real capabilities for us to contribute meaningfully to this conversation.

As for your question on whether Singapore will one day have a Parliament without parties, I have also been thinking about this question very seriously. In today's world, how will this system look like and how does it work? Traditionally, people have parties because they have a certain frame — a party manifesto, party positions, and they ask people to vote along those lines. But it's a very interesting proposition. The question is not so much whether we will have a Parliament without any parties. The question is more of a second order question which I alluded to in one of my hypotheses, even assuming that we do away with this political parties structure where everybody stand on their own as individuals, independent right, in the respective place. The question then is, how do we bring people together for action?

How do we bring about convergence? Now, I don't yet have a final answer to your question because I think these are things that we need to think about very seriously. That's why in my hypothesis I say, in today's world, a lot of people focus on the first part. How to generate diversity, how to generate debate? Those are all very good. After all the debate and discussion, how do we bring people together?

On data

Q: Hello, I'm Goh Meng Seng, People's Power Party. It's quite refreshing to hear that you actually wanted deep level debate about policies, I welcome that. But maybe this is the new 4G leaders who are more open. But as an opponent of PAP where we have been always chasing PAP Ministers for public debate about policies, we face rejection. So I hope that in the coming election, I should not face such a rejection. Before we can have a deep debate of anything, data, statistics are important. Now, a lot of people are mistaken that oppositions are opportunist, we do not know our stuff, we do not know policy options, which is not true. What we lack is data, statistics. And only with that, we can actually do our own analysis and come up with our own policy options. Then we can have a meaningful debate. I'm an economics student from the 1990s. I have difficulties of having raw data that I can look at and come up with a meaningful thesis. It is possible to get data from SingStat, but we have to do a lot of mining. A lot of calculation, deduction and all that but in doing so, any assumption that we make in our deduction will actually contaminate the data, and it's not accurate. It can only be an estimate and it is not very helpful if you are going to talk about deep debate, policy debate about that.

Chan Chun Sing:

Now, I think the issue goes beyond data sharing. Actually Meng Seng, I wasn't sure exactly what you were trying to get us to do. Because you say that you wanted raw data. Then you say that you have to do a lot of work with raw data. But if we give raw data then you will need to do some work with raw data. But if we give you the conclusion then you might be suspicious as to how we draw the conclusion. So I'm not exactly sure whether you prefer raw data or you prefer processed data.

But let me say this. Data is not the panacea to everything. Beyond just the provision of data, there are two or three other important aspects when it comes to this. Number one, all of us have a responsibility to check our confirmation bias. We can have a lot of data, but if we go in, with a preconceived idea on what the data should tell us, and we have a confirmation bias, we will go and interpret it in a way that we believe. In fact, recently we had a very simple case whereby the data was available but people chose to truncate the graph, and then came up with a different conclusion. Entirely possible. So it's not just about data. Data is necessary, but we also need to have an enquiring mind and be open to ask what the data tells us and how do we interpret this. You can have the same data but all I'm cautioning here is that unless we go in with no preconceived ideas and learn to interpret it, having data alone is insufficient.

Then there's a third point. Even if we have the data and interpreted the data, there must be some level of trust. At the end of the day, you can tell people a lot of data, but from my own experience, if people don't trust you as a person, you can give as much data as you want, and you will not win over the hearts nor the minds of the person. In fact, for many of the questions that we are confronting with, I don't think it is an issue of the data per se. Of course data helps. But at the end of the day, when we go out to confront many of these issues, we have to also have that trust. It is not data alone that will convince our people what are the choices. It is also about the trust that our people have with us. Without that trust, nothing will work very much.

In fact, today if you go onto the internet, whenever the data comes out, there will be the following categories of reaction. There will be one small group, a very small group that says "Are you sure your data is correct?" That's the first reaction. Then the second group, which is not bad, will ask "Is this the only way to interpret the data?" which is okay. But at the end of the day, how you win the hearts and the minds of people has to go beyond data. You look back at our first and second generation of leaders. I don't think it is just data alone that won them over, but it is because of what they say, what they deliver that earn the trust and therefore people go along with them.

On activism and values

Q: I am Mathew Ting from the China Foundation. My question is on the core values. I mean, has any of the political parties in Singapore, whether it's the incumbent or the opposition, come out to say what are their core values, this is what we stand for, and you know, when you go for an election, this is what you should consider when voting. So then, all the other things become you know, points of debate, frivolous, whatever, what really matters is the fundamentals, this is our stand, this is what we do not compromise on and this is what we are, and maybe around the pledge or something like that, as the core values of Singaporeans.

Bilahari Kausikan:

I think Singapore's official core value is multi-racial meritocracy, and I don't think anybody, opposition or government, would overtly deny that there is a core value. However, that comes into conflict with other values, there is never only one value, you know? And what is the mixture, is in the cases of some opposition, a little bit fuzzy, to my mind at least, I may be wrong but to me it's a bit fuzzy, because electoral imperative may also bring you away from your core values.

Lam Peng Er:

When we look at the opposition parties, I don't think any of them would campaign against meritocracy, multi-culturalism and so on. Not to be cruel to the Workers' Party, because Pritam Singh was my student at NUS, I like him, but you look at the Workers' Party, it's a bluer shade of white. What are they arguing — that hey, we need checks and balances in Singapore, right? You have to deny the PAP a more than two-thirds majority so that they cannot change the constitution. So that's their argument, they are not arguing against the core values, the template set by the founding fathers, by Mr Lee Kuan Yew and the Lieutenants.

> When we look at the opposition parties, I don't think any of them would campaign against meritocracy, multi-culturalism and so on...what they are arguing is that we need checks and balance in Singapore.
>
> — *Lam Peng Er*

Zuraidah Ibrahim:

On core values, I think Singapore is very fortunate that thanks to our founding fathers, there is a certain threshold of what acceptable values are and what values that we frown upon are. As a minority, I think the core value of multi-racialism is important. Over the years, the core value of inclusivity is important. I think the debate is not over the core values that we have, but the debate should be the commitment to which we stick to these core values and how prepared we are to re-examine them at different points of our existence as a nation. I am not so sure we

> I think the debate is not over the core values that we have, but the debate should be the commitment to which we stick to these core values and how prepared we are to re-examine them at different points of our existence as a nation.
>
> — *Zuraidah Ibrahim*

have done enough of that, but I think we are starting off on a very good footing where there is broad consensus, we are not a polarised society, we are not divided by these core values, so that's something positive for us. And I do think that DPM Heng's slogan of "Singapore Together" can resonate if it's fleshed out meaningfully.

Q: My name is Ian and I am from the Raffles Institution. I will start with the assumption that Singaporean students are largely non or apolitical, and it seems to me that these days, the government seems more enthusiastic about youth caring more about issues in our society, and actually going about championing them. However, I was just curious, how do you think the government would react if this activism sort of spilled over into the politicisation of students, especially if this politicisation takes an anti-establishment stance. And do you think the government will be accepting of these new forms of student activism. Thank you.

Zuraidah Ibrahim:
I don't think the Singapore establishment has made any bones or been apologetic about the fact that if you are studying, you should be studying; politics should be a bit further from your mind. But at the same time, I don't think they have been so intolerant as to not allow speakers or to allow some form of activity by students. But I think again, if I can just anticipate what was beneath that question, that's really to compare student activism in Hong Kong versus in Singapore.

I think student activism in Hong Kong, I sometimes think that it's mother's milk, because since 1997 Hong Kongers have only known one major way of making their views heard and that is going out to the streets. So, in 2003, you had them going out to the streets and Article 23 which was, which is a piece of legislation that pertains to national security, was aborted, shelved. 2012, again, you had Hong Kongers going out to the streets to protest against the changes to the national curriculum. Again, that was shelved and then 2014, you had the Occupy Movement, that was in protest against a framework that was meant to give universal suffrage to Hong Kong. Again, that was rejected.

And now you have these protests that have continued for eight months, I don't think that protest mindset will go away any time soon. I think it will wax and wane depending on some sort of agreement that both sides come to; it can well be a war of attrition, it can well be some sort of basic understanding, and it can also have to do with the wider public. I got the sense that over Christmas actually, the majority of Hong Kongers who actually are solidly behind the protests, were getting a bit weary of the protests. So, there was a bit of a period of calm, whether that calm will last, that was broken yesterday, whether it will prevail in the coming weeks and months, we shall have to see.

Bilahari Kausikan:

On whether the Singapore government can tolerate greater politicisation of students. Well, it really depends what you mean by politicisation. If you get involved more in debating issues, speaking about issues, I think there will be that tolerance. If you get involved in the way Hong Kong students are getting involved, by breaking things in the street, I think there will be zero tolerance. And that brings me to a different point about core values. It is not so much whether you agree with the core values or not, it's how you, what your vision is of implementing them.

> And that brings me to a different point about core values. It is not so much whether you agree with the core values or not, it's how you, what your vision is of implementing them.
> — *Bilahari Kausikan*

Similarly, when you criticise or you get politicized, it's not just a matter of saying white when the government says black. You have to have some viable alternative. Like for example, I think in Hong Kong, all the five demands of the protestors cannot be met, and I don't think the protesters are so silly to think that they can be met. It's really, to my mind — and Zuraidah will know better because she lives there, working for Jack Ma — it is really a deep sense of frustration and in fact, almost desperation. That does not exist in Singapore, so if you want to be politicised, you have to come up with better governance solutions. Otherwise, if you think the role of a political opposition is merely to cry black when the government says white, or to ensure the government will not get a blank cheque without viable alternatives, it reminds me very much of what Dr Mahathir said after the last General Election. He said, "I didn't expect to win, so I don't have to keep all my promises."

So there are young people in the government who are stakeholders in different facets of society, the government also does cooperate with many other organisations in civil society that have active young people participating. You probably ask more questions than any other people who are maybe twice or three times your age. So keep doing that because I really enjoy how you are not yet jaded or have not yet internalised OB markers. Sometimes the questions you ask may feel like a bit very blatant or in-your-face, but it's perhaps because the adults don't feel like we should ask the same questions anymore, so keep being young and keep being angry productively!

— *Crystal Abidin*

Q: Do you feel that the government is doing enough to hear the views of young people or just the general public on issues that they are passionate about, like for example through memes or social media, or are young people and the general public doing enough to express their views to the government and like what do you think could be done to bridge the gap between the government and the people?

Crystal Abidin:

Is the government doing enough to hear the views of the young people? Are young people doing enough to be heard by the government? Number one, there are young people in the government. We use the term "millennials" quite loosely. I feel that these days we use the term millennials as a scapegoat, anti-label to refer to young people who are noisy and troublesome because we don't understand them. But if you are really talking about millennials as a generational cohort, these are your people in your mid-20s to mid-30s. If you are talking about younger people who may spend a lot of time on social media, these are your Gen Zs who grew up online.

So there are young people in the government who are stakeholders in different facets of society, the government also does cooperate with many other organisations in civil society that have active young people participating. You probably ask more questions than any other people who are maybe twice or three times your age. So keep doing that because I really enjoy how you are not yet jaded or have not yet internalised OB markers. Sometimes the questions you ask may feel like a bit very blatant or in-your-face, but it's perhaps because the adults don't feel like we should ask the same questions anymore, so keep being young and keep being angry productively!

Carrie Tan:

I really like Crystal's point here about young people being angry productively. I think this keyword here is "being angry productively". I think there are plenty of channels for all parts of society to listen to young people and I think the government has done a pretty good job of offering up these avenues and channels and platforms. But I think myself being "not-so-young young person", I'm kind of like on the borderline with the elder Millennial, my encouragement or suggestion to younger people following my cohort is that there is a difference between airing your views as an angsty young person and airing your views as an informed, matured, balanced young person.

> There is a difference between airing your views as an angsty young person and airing your views as an informed, matured, balanced young person.
>
> — *Carrie Tan*

I think you know that there are opportunities for many of us to get proactively involved in some of the issues and causes that we care about. I believe in service with informed views. That you know, you need to kind of roll up your sleeves and get down the mud and really get a very close sense of working on the issues in order to have a much more mature and informed views of these issues.

And this is my personal journey from being angry about "how come the government is not doing enough for poverty" to now moderating my views. It is not because you know, I changed my mind but because I understand the complexity so much more after working on the ground. And I think this makes a difference between anyone sharing views in person or audience listening to it whether they want to or they are able to take their views and translate them into implementable actions.

Q: I'm Zanul Abidin, I'm amazed at the eloquence and the articulateness of the panel. My question is in talking about values, I was placing myself 50 years back, 40 years back when I was their age. I shared the same concerns but I never thought in terms of the intergenerational problems, I just did what I needed to do in terms of social work or social services helping bridge the gaps between the society, in the society. So my question is, what is your response to people like me, like us, the older generation. There's little chance of them actually riding on the internet or the social media. Do you just ignore us? Or how do you respond to people like us to imbibe your values?

Lastrina Hamid:

If I could share one example that's happening at home, my father remarried about two years ago and I was trying to find ways on how I can talk to my stepmom — she's Indonesian — on you know, recycling. And I didn't really want to go into details and tell her you know like Singapore has a waste management problem and so on. But really I was just showing her what was happening, that on the void deck, we have a blue bin, someone comes in and collects all these recyclable materials. At home, I'm going to put this plastic here, you know, if you can, whenever we have cans or plastic bottles, can you put it in the plastic. I think that kind of direct, simple conversations with people of the older generation is something that I find has been working for me in terms of communicating my point across.

> I think that kind of direct, simple conversations with people of the older generation is something that I find has been working for me in terms of communicating my point across.
>
> — *Lastrina Hamid*

If I may just add another layer to that — how I'm also engaging people of the younger generation. So I have a five-and-a-half-year-old niece, she doesn't understand all these social media stuff. We go out quite often and I bring her, you know, from Hort Park all the way to Harbourfront. And it's a very long walk. She's very tired. But she's exposed to the outdoors and we get to talk about a lot of things about nature. And I think that's also another way for me at least to engage people of the younger generation and tell them more about environmental protection and conservation conversation. It's through bringing them outdoors.

Crystal Abidin:

The common response is always to find common ground right, between the young and the old. And this has also become an empty signifier, what is the common ground. As an anthropologist, I find that the best way to understand people is not to bring them together for a specific cause, but to let them spend time together. You cannot just throw people into a room and say, okay what in our lives intersect on the Venn diagram, let's "extremely bond" on this, and now let's "extremely persuade" each other about this specific issue. I think if you want to groom empathy and understanding, you naturally have to spend time with people. Like the way Yinzhou, Lastrina and Carrie have being doing with the groups that they are working with. You cannot just parachute yourself into a group and say you are going to be an advocate.

If I were to give an advice to young people, it will be to build allies. Not just allies horizontally in your generation across different advocacy and causes, but vertical allies. These days, whenever there is a social movement in Singapore, when it first starts, we are all energised, we are so excited it is going viral, great. Many days of sustenance in this and then we lose stamina and that's it. So in order for a lot of these movements to take root deeply and to have impact, we want to reflect on history. What have people before us done? Even if we are talking about social media or new phenomenon, nothing is really new in this world.

It's important to see what our forefathers have done, whether or not we agreed or disagreed with them, in order to build stamina, to add on to our action, we want generational allies back to the people who have gone before us. And I don't say this as lip service just to honour all the people; 80% of you are probably older than us here in this panel. But the fact is that we sometimes tend to do the same things over and over without consolidating, we put them on different avenues, we do not remember, we do not seek to think and review what has come before us. And as a young person, with probably a lot of energy, I think that will be one of the earliest steps for us to consider.

Q: My question is directed to Mr Cai Yinzhou. Thank you for sharing with us how you tried to change the narrative that we carry with us about foreign migrant workers. My question is to flip it around the other way and say could you share with us the narratives that foreign migrant workers have about Singapore. What sort of narratives do they have and what do they say about us as a society? Thank you.

Cai Yinzhou:

So thank you for that question on how foreign workers view Singaporeans. Now that's an interesting question because for many of the foreign workers, what they share is mostly what we have heard. Like how Singapore is very good, there is good transportation, good safety, a lot of it speaking in comparison with their countries back home, the lives they have left to come here. However, I think the next step as we probe further is often like what your future plans will be. Many of them have the impression that being a low-wage foreign worker, it is also completely impossible for them to imagine settling down here. So one of the perspectives that I have heard is, "You know, my dream is to become Singaporean." Unfortunately the truth is, unless you have enough money, or you have enough certification or enough credibility, it will be hard to even dream about that.

The other thing that migrant workers have shared with me is also how much of what I have taken for granted personally. Many of them share about the struggles that they have made to come here, and it does remind me of stories, similar stories that we have read about in history, even hearing from my grandfather himself who came to Singapore from China. So that I think was a point of reflection where many of them, what they are going through right now, coming to a foreign land to work, if they ever get injured or they meet a salary problem or if they have a bad boss, who do they really turn to. And if I were speaking about it from my grandfather's point of view, I would hope that the local community would be the one that rallies around to help them in times of need. And I think that perspective really got me to think about foreign workers in Singapore and not just thinking of them as people outside of us but people who really we have a lot to learn from as well.

The advice that I would give to passionate youths is really to find out and be curious. The fire that Crystal mentioned most young people have and eventually lose when they join the workforce or they become jaded, is really true. And many students who I have met who are passionate about the projects that they are given to do, they sometimes approach it from a frame of what's the process that I have been taught. What's the design thinking methodology? What's the kind of points that I hope to get and the metrics that I should use to measure that. And unfortunately that stifles a lot of what is possible for many of these passionate students.

I think one point of encouragement also for fellow educators is to sometimes having an open frame of allowing them to immerse themselves not just with migrant workers but also for us with elderly. For example in nursing homes, a group of Cedar students who came by, just spend three hours with them over a month, every week, just mingling around and chilling out with elderly. The ideas that they thought about were completely out of the box. And a lot of designs came from the perspectives of the conversations that they have. I thought that was a very beautiful process that the teacher was open enough to let them take through, that was really encouraging for passionate youths to continue that fire through others, through the education and mentorship of teachers and external partners.

About the Contributors

CAI Yinzhou is the Director of Citizen Adventures Private Limited, a company that aims to bridge gaps between disadvantaged communities and formal structures by encouraging sustainable models for self-organised groups. Starting from 2013, notable social initiatives by his company include Geylang Adventures, Dakota Adventures tours and #backalleybarbers. To date, the team at #backalleybarbers has given more than 3,000 free haircuts to people on the streets of Geylang, nursing homes, migrant worker shelters and rental flat communities. Through the tours and other social initiatives, he hopes to inspire collective action for positive societal change.

CHAN Chun Sing is the current Minister for Trade and Industry, Minister-In-Charge for the Public Service, and Second Assistant Secretary-General for the governing People's Action Party. Mr Chan is also Deputy Chairman of the People's Association and the Member of Parliament for the Tanjong Pagar Group Representation Constituency. Mr Chan's previous appointments included Minister in the Prime Minister's Office and Secretary-General of the National Trades Union Congress. Mr Chan also served as Minister for Social and Family Development (MSF) and Second Minister for Defence. His other previous appointments included Acting Minister for Community Development, Youth and Sports, and Minister of State for Information, Communications and the Arts). Mr Chan served with the Singapore Armed Forces (SAF) from 1987 to 2011. He held various appointments, including Chief of Army (2010 to 2011), Chief of Staff, Joint Staff (2009 to 2010) and Commander 9th Division / Chief Infantry Officer (2007 to 2009). Educated at the Raffles Institution (1982 to 1985) and Raffles Junior College (1986 to 1987), Mr Chan was awarded the SAF (Overseas) and President's Scholarship to study Economics at Christ's College, Cambridge University in the United

Kingdom in 1988 and graduated with First Class Honours. Mr Chan was awarded the Distinguished Master Strategist Award 1998 by the US Army Command and General Staff College. In 2005, he completed the Sloan Fellows Programme at the Massachusetts Institute of Technology under the Lee Kuan Yew Scholarship.

CRYSTAL Abidin is a digital anthropologist and ethnographer of vernacular internet cultures. She researches internet celebrity, influencer cultures, and social media pop cultures. Her published books include Internet Celebrity: Understanding Fame Online (2018, Emerald Publishing), Microcelebrity Around the Globe: Approaches to Cultures of Internet Fame (2018, Emerald Publishing, co-edited with Megan Lindsay Brown), Instagram: Visual Social Media Cultures (2020, Polity Press, co-authored with Tama Leaver and Tim Highfield), Mediated Interfaces: The Body on Social Media (2020, Bloomsbury Academic, co-edited with Katie Warfield and Carolina Cambre), and tumblr (2021, Polity Press, co-authored with Katrin Tiidenberg and Natalie Ann Hendry). Crystal's forthcoming books investigate the history of Singaporean blogshops as youth-driven DIY e-commerce, the influencer industry and shifting trends over a decade, and emergent youth cultures on TikTok. A graduate of the National University of Singapore and University of Western Australia, she is currently Associate Professor of Internet Studies and Australian Research Council (ARC) Discovery Early Career Researcher Award (DECRA) Fellow at Curtin University. On top of being an authority in social media and society studies, she is listed on ABC Top 5 Humanities Fellows (2020), Forbes 30 Under 30 Asia (2018), and Pacific Standard 30 Top Thinkers Under 30 (2016).

DEVAN, Janadas, Director of the Institute of Policy Studies, was educated at the National University of Singapore and Cornell University in the United States. He was a journalist, writing for The Straits Times and broadcasting for Radio Singapore International, before being appointed the Government's Chief of Communications at the Ministry of Communications and Information in 2012. He is concurrently Deputy Secretary at the Prime Minister's Office.

FARISH Ahmad-Noor is Associate Professor and Coordinator of the PhD programme at the S. Rajaratnam School of International Studies and the School of History at Nanyang Technological University (NTU). Associate Professor Farish received his Bachelor of Arts in Philosophy and Literature from the University of Sussex in 1989, before studying for a Masters of Arts in Philosophy at the same University in 1990 and a Masters in South-East Asian Studies at the School of Oriental and African Studies, University of London. He completed his PhD at the University of Essex in 1997 in the field of governance and politics. He is a political historian and his main area of research has been Southeast Asia in the 19th century. Dubbed the "rock star professor" by The Star, he has a well-established media profile and has hosted several CNA documentaries on Southeast Asia.

HENG Swee Keat is Singapore's Deputy Prime Minister, Coordinating Minister for Economic Policies, Minister for Finance and Member of Parliament for East Coast GRC. As Minister for Finance, Mr Heng oversees the revenue and expenditure policy of Singapore, and the allocation of resources to achieve national security, economic and social objectives. Mr Heng also chairs the tripartite Future Economy Council which oversees the on-going restructuring of our economy, through upgrading of the skills of our workers and the transformation of industry, to create even better careers prospects for our people. He leads a team to oversee the design and implementation of national strategies in areas such as skills and capabilities development, innovation and productivity and the internationalisation of our companies. Mr Heng chairs the National Research Foundation, which sets the direction for Singapore's research, innovation and enterprise strategies. In this role, he brings together the universities and research communities with businesses to create a more vibrant innovation ecosystem. Mr Heng also serves as Adviser to the Multi-Ministry Taskforce on COVID-19 and the National Jobs Council. Mr Heng has an MA in Economics from Cambridge University. He also holds a Master in Public Administration from the Kennedy School of Government, Harvard University.

KAUSIKAN, Bilahari is currently Chairman of the Middle East Institute, an autonomous institute of the National University of Singapore. He has spent his entire career in the Ministry of Foreign Affairs before retiring as

Ambassador-at-Large in 2018. During his 37 years in the Ministry, he served in a variety of appointments at home and abroad, including as the Second Permanent Secretary and Permanent Secretary. Raffles Institution, the University of Singapore and Columbia University in New York all attempted to educate him.

LAM Peng Er is Principal Research Fellow at National University of Singapore (NUS) East Asian Institute, and was previously part of the NUS Department of Political Science. He obtained his PhD in Political Science from Columbia University and has written widely, with a particular interest in Japanese and Singaporean politics. He was a co-editor of Lee's Lieutenants: Singapore's Old Guard (1999), a seminal volume on Singapore's first generation of political leaders. Dr Lam's academic publications have appeared in international journals such as the Pacific Affairs, Asian Survey, Asian Affairs, Japan Forum, and Government and Opposition. He is an executive editor of the International Relations of the Asia-Pacific (a journal of the Japan Association of International Relations published by Oxford University Press) and Asian Journal of Peacebuilding (of the Institute for Peace and Unification Studies, Seoul National University).

NOR LASTRINA Hamid is an environmental activist and co-founder of Singapore Youth for Climate Action — a network of Singaporeans working for climate action. In 2015, she had the honour of being the voice of YOUNGO (Youth Non-Governmental Organisations) — a youth constituency of the United Nations Framework Convention on Climate Change (UNFCCC) — at the 21st United Nations negotiations on climate change under the UNFCCC framework in Paris. At the United Nations conference, she urged all nations to commit and take action against climate change. Ms Nor Lastrina has done voluntary work to help the environment since 2009 and is the recipient of the National Environmental Agency NEA EcoFriend Awards 2016.

TAN, Carrie is a Singaporean politician and serves as a Member of Parliament of Nee Soon GRC. Prior to joining politics, Carrie founded Daughters Of Tomorrow, where she is now a Strategic Advisor, a non-profit organization which enables livelihoods and financial self-sufficiency for low-income women in Singapore. She is passionate about improving social mobility for families in poverty. Carrie is also a champion for improving labour conditions, enabling families through enhanced caregiving support, and change-making through civic participation and community collaboration.

TAN Tai Yong is President and Professor of Humanities (History) at Yale-NUS College. Professor Tan was the National University of Singapore's Vice-Provost (Student Life) overseeing all student matters in the university. He also served as Dean of the Faculty of Arts and Social Sciences and was the founding Director of the Institute of South Asian Studies (ISAS). A member of the NUS Department of History since 1992, he specialises in South and Southeast Asian History and has published extensively on the Sikh diaspora, the social and political history of colonial Punjab, decolonisation and the partition of South Asia, and Singapore history. Professor Tan is Honorary Chairman of the National Museum of Singapore and Chairman of the National Heritage Board's National Collection Advisory Panel. He was also a member of the Singapore Bicentennial Advisory Panel, and served as a Nominated Member of Parliament from 2014 to 2015.

ZURAIDAH Ibrahim is Deputy Executive Editor of the South China Morning Post (SCMP). She oversees Hong Kong and Asia coverage and is also editor of This Week in Asia, SCMP's award-winning weekly magazine focusing on regional current affairs. Prior to this, she was Deputy Editor of The Straits Times (2010 to 2014) before leaving for Hong Kong in December 2014. Ms Zuraidah is a co-author of Lee Kuan Yew: Hard Truths to Keep Singapore Going (2011), based on lengthy interviews with the late founding father as well as Opposition (2016), which examines the history and prospects of Singapore's opposition parties. A student of political science, she commutes between Hong Kong and Singapore, writing extensively about politics in Asia.

9 789811 225727